NINE SOVIET PORTRAITS

NINE SOVIET PORTRAITS

RAYMOND A. BAUER

with the assistance of
EDWARD WASIOLEK

GREENWOOD PRESS, PUBLISHERS
WESTPORT, CONNECTICUT

Library of Congress Cataloging in Publication Data

Bauer, Raymond Augustine, 1916-
    Nine Soviet portraits.

    Reprint of the 1965 ed. published by the M.I.T.
Press, Cambridge, Mass.
    1. Russians. 2. Russia--Social conditions--
1945-   3. Russia--Social life and customs--1917-
1970. 4. National characteristics, Russian.
I. Wasiolek, Edward, joint author. II. Title.
[DK33.B37 1979]   947   79-4609
ISBN 0-313-20929-4

Reprinted in 1979 by Greenwood Press, Inc.
51 Riverside Avenue, Westport, CT 06880

Printed in the United States of America

10 9 8 7 6 5 4 3 2 1

Foreword

This book was done on a dare. Several years ago Walt W. Rostow asked me to prepare a set of synthetic portraits of "typical Soviet types" in connection with a study of Soviet society which he was conducting for the Center for International Studies at M.I.T. His request almost took the form of a challenge, and if I remember his words they went like this: "You psychologists and sociologists [since I am a social psychologist he applied both terms of abuse to me] are good at taking people apart. You do a fine job of analyzing people's behavior until it's reduced to a set of abstractions. But can you put a person back together again and give somebody an idea of what these abstractions mean in terms of the day to day experiences of a real, living person— instead of graphs, statistics, and generalizations?" The present book is the result of my attempt to meet this challenge. I have tried in these nine sketches to convey the life situation of a group of "typical" Soviet citizens, what they do, what happens to them, how they feel about it, and what sorts of persons they are.

The sources of information which were used, and the way in which Mr. Wasiolek and I went about this job, are all described in some detail in the Appendix. As you will see from the Appendix, these sketches are intended to convey in fictional form a fairly systematic set of propositions about Soviet society. For the sake of those of you who want to get on with the stories and don't like reading appendixes anyway, I would mention that the

v

main source of information for these stories—though certainly not the only one—is a series of several hundreds of interviews with former Soviet citizens which were conducted in Europe and America by the Harvard Project on the Soviet Social System of which I was a member.

A fair number of Soviet terms have been retained in their original forms because they lose a good deal of flavor on being rendered into English. Thus, "Secretary of the Raion Party Committee" lacks entirely the snap of the typically Soviet contraction *Raikomsec.* The Glossary on p. 189 explains them.

RAYMOND A. BAUER

Center for International Studies
Massachusetts Institute of Technology
1955

Preface to Paperback Edition

For practical purposes, *Nine Soviet Portraits* was written ten years ago. Like most authors, I have not been able to refrain from looking back at my earlier work with mixed feelings — critically, approvingly, quizzically. Perhaps a baring of some of these feelings may provide guidance to the reader of the paperback edition.

There is, first of all, the matter of the fictional form of these portraits. While I wrote as well as I could, neither then nor now have I had any illusion but that the fictional form was a device for meeting the challenge of my sponsor, Walt W. Rostov, to "put people back together." Having a moderately well developed critical appreciation of good writing, I quickly realized my primary commitment had to be to the content and not to form. The alternative was to give up. *The New Yorker* quipped that I wrote fiction like a social psychologist — so there you have it.

So much for form. Now for the more important matter of substance.

Admittedly, almost all of this material pertains to the Stalin era, with only the Party Secretary, as something of an exception, being concerned with the post-Stalin succession crisis. At the time of publication, there were some friends who thought I possibly overstressed certain conditions: food, clothing, and especially housing shortages; mismanagement of collective farms; the extent of political terror; and the prevalence of extralegal practices in industry. Fortunately, the necessity for documenting these points is now less urgent due to the appearance on the scene of a vigorous, although unanticipated collaborator: Nikita S. Khrushchev. As far as critical statements concerning the Stalin period are concerned, they have by now been pretty well accepted in current Soviet sources — although subject to occasional cyclical reverses and modification. The still skeptical reader is referred to Khrushchev's speeches. During my visit to the U.S.S.R., I was on several occasions asked if I had written critically about the Soviet Union. My stock reply was: "I have said nothing that Khrushchev has not said, but perhaps I erred by saying it first."

There have been changes since Stalin's death, some of them quite important. Certainly the most striking of these is the relaxation of the rule of police terror. Hopefully these portraits, by showing the pervasiveness of this terror under Stalin, will give the reader a better appreciation of why the post-Stalin leaders moved to reduce this source of intense anxiety and hostility. There is perennial talk of a tendency to revert to "Stalinism" — a statement which may mean a variety of things. However, as far as the system of police terror is concerned, the testimony of exceeedingly well qualified visitors to the Soviet Union is that there is a general desire even in fairly high places to develop a system of legal constraints that would prevent the recurrence of a system of terror. This is especially true of leading Soviet jurists who are attempting to develop codes to deal with this problem.

Certain other issues persist in altered form. The standard of living has improved, but the regime still fails signally to meet the rising expectations of the public. Khrushchev's failure to come close to his own announced goals for agriculture is the topic of wide discussion in the West. Continued discussion of this issue in the Soviet press and the speeches of high officials suggest this will be a continuing though diminishing problem.

In any event, the agricultural problem has not been solved. And the collective farm is still bedeviled by the problems of poor adminstration, poor motivation for the peasantry, underinvestment, personal conniving, and neglect of repairs of machinery.

The dissatisfaction of creative artists with Stalinesque regimentation is depicted in the portrait of the creative writer. The most casual reading of the current press indicates what a live issue this has been between the regime and the various groups of artists: novelists, poets, painters, film makers. Perhaps it is this running controversy more than any other issue that precipitates speculation of a "return to Stalinism." It is my considered opinion that rather than "return to Stalin" the regime will continue alternately to grant and withdraw privileges in a fitful and sometimes irascible fashion, but that over the next several years a pattern will shake out that will be immensely more liberal than could have been hoped for under Stalin.

I suppose any writer whose wildest speculation is unequivocally verified finds it irresistible to cite the confirming evidence even if it reduces the suspense of his own work.

My guiding rule in writing the *Portraits* was to curb any major flights of imagination and use only themes and incidents for which Edward Wasiolek or I could find at least a close approximation in some responsible source. My one burst of self-indulgence was the final section of the portrait of the creative writer. In this section I had the writer produce an allegory of his own frustrated situation and have it published as an allegory of the plight of the manual laborer under capitalism. His allegory received fine critical acclaim and was widely sold. A limited group, however, laughed privately because they understood the true meaning of the allegory.

I was quite pleased, but even more surprised, to find that a virtually identical event had actually happened among Hungarian writers after the Revolution of 1956. (See "Hungarian Writers Balk," *The Christian Science Monitor,* October 13, 1958. Note the following passage:

> The motto given was the conventional socialist one of weakness in isolation, contrasted with strength in solidarity. But most of Mr. Tamazi's readers took his story as he had doubtless intended it — an allegory showing the plight of Hungary's persecuted writers themselves.

Verification of a single point could be a trivial matter. What is at stake is the nature of *the mechanisms of accommodation which people adopt in an "impossible" situation.* This is the essence of *Nine Soviet Portraits.* It is in effect a nonpolitical approach to a highly political situation. Writings about Soviet totalitarianism a decade or so ago could easily create the impression that nobody could conceivably live in such a situation. My job was to show how this was possible.

Once more I have received welcome confirmation from a Soviet source. In 1962, Alexander Solzhenitsyn wrote and published in the Soviet Union the "novel" *One Day in the Life of Ivan Denisovich* (translated and published in the United States by Praeger). Mr. Solzhenitsyn, a former labor camp inmate himself, drew a "portrait" of a labor camp inmate. The curious reader ought to read this book. We may assume that Solzhenitsyn is an adequate authority on the subjective world of labor camp inmates. It was therefore gratifying to find what in my judgment was such close confirmation of what we had been able to infer from much poorer sources of information — and fortunately were able to publish much earlier.

Unquestionably there are errors of both fact and emphasis. The one point on which I have most retrospective doubt is the anxiety of subordinates in the presence of superiors in the factory and on the collective farm. This comes from having toured a collective farm and a number of factories. This issue was brought home most forcibly when the chief engineer of a large factory and I tried to fight our way through a door while the day-shift workers rushed out of the shop on the way to the locker room. The fact that we were dressed in suits and were "big shots" struck home not at all.

On the whole, however, I remained convinced that the *Portraits* are a fruitful source for understanding present-day Soviet society. The changes that have taken place have taken place against the background of the Stalin era, and there are few instances of which I know where the original state of affairs does not remain at least as a nagging issue in the background.

In retrospect I have come to appreciate increasingly the wisdom of Walt W. Rostow's notion of "putting people back together." Science is of necessity based on abstractions and generalizations. But, what is lost in such abstractions as "socialist totalitarianism" is not mere idiosyncratic anecdotal material of conversational interest. What happens "inside the categories" is the source of change. While originally I thought of the *Portraits* as a study of *how individuals live* in a totalitarian society, I have come increasingly to think of concrete data of this sort as a source for understanding the dynamics of a society.

Finally, may I once more pay tribute to my collaborator, Edward Wasiolek, for having so capably steered me in fruitful directions and kept me out of trouble.

Cambridge, Massachusetts   RAYMOND A. BAUER
December, 1964

Contents

NINE SOVIET PORTRAITS

— Well, Mama, what institute did I get into? Or did I fail again?

Krokodil.

The Students

Stepan Ivanovitch Gravinov bent over his notebook, making a last-minute review of his notes on the significance of Belinsky in the development of nineteenth-century revolutionary literature. The notebook was propped against the pile of books, newspapers, and journals stacked on the back of the table for want of any other place to put them.

Pavel Pavlovitch Zagordi, his roommate, began rummaging through the pile and almost set everything tumbling. Each braced the pile with one hand while trying to reestablish some semblance of balance by rearranging the stack with the other.

"What were you looking for, Pavel?" Stepan asked.

"That crib on Pushkin that I borrowed from Samigin. I have to get through this exam with a five or at least a four."

"But, Pavel, didn't you give that to Vera last week?"

"Oh, yeh, that's right. What the hell will I do now? Hey, I'll tell you what. You bone me up on Pushkin on the way over to the exam, and I'll coach you on dialectical materialism tomorrow night before the exam in diamat."

Stepan closed his notebook quietly and smiled at Pavel.

"All right, I guess I would be better off if I stopped cramming now. If I don't know nineteenth-century Russian literature by now I'll never know anything. Come on, let's go."

They slipped on their coats and left the dormitory, walking

slowly in the direction of the auditorium in which the exam was being held.

As they walked along Stepan recited briefly the salient facts of Pushkin's life, his outstanding works, his position in world literature, his importance to the development of present-day Soviet literature. After each few sentences he would pause to let Pavel repeat after him. It was obvious that Pavel knew only the barest facts about Pushkin; and the coaching was, if anything, only confusing him more.

"Oh, the Devil take Pushkin, and the venerable Professor A. A. Gorovin too. Forget it, Stepanushka. If I'm lucky and get a question that I know, I'll get by. Otherwise I'm sunk." Pavel sighed.

Stepan looked at him walking along in silence. Pavel's worry did not take the cockiness out of his rolling gait. Even in despair he always maintained the self-assurance of a Moscow wise-guy who knew all the ropes and was confident that by some means he would get what he was after.

What a queer pair we make, thought Stepan. . . . They had met in the Army, when Pavel had "adopted" the bookish peasant lad who was so quiet, studious, likable, friendly, but just didn't know his way around. After the war they had both decided to go back to school, and here they were in the Pedagogical Institute studying together.

"Pavel, don't you care enough to study?"

"Don't I care? Boy, how can you ask a goofy question like that? Look, you know just as well as I do the fix I'm in. I don't want to end up teaching third grade out in some little hick town. If it wasn't for my background I would have gone into the heavy-machinery institute. Boy, if I don't crack this exam I won't get my stipend next year. And that's where I'll be—teaching third grade."

They were silent again for a while. Then Stepan spoke up once more.

"Look, Pavel, it's your own business. But you would be a lot better off if you spent more time in studying rather than doing so much social work. Look at yesterday afternoon. You could have skipped that Komsomol meeting. It was a general meeting, and nobody would have missed you. I've missed four general meetings this year and the Secretary never mentioned it. I'll bet he never even noticed it."

"Not if *you* missed it, boy. But if *I* missed it, that would be different. Supposing I'm going to teach Russian literature to a lot of middle-school students. Why should I crack my head about Gogol's realism, or the meaning of Pushkin's *Freedom?* I bone up with a couple of official interpretations from the literary journals. Who are you kidding? Do you think that all those evenings you spend with old Gorovin are going to do you any good? When you get to teaching you'll have to follow the official outline like everybody e¹se. If old Pavel is going to get any place it's through the Komsomol and the Party. Do you think the Director of the Institute is a whizz on pedagogical theory or Russian literature? Don't worry about me, Stepanush, old boy."

Pavel again, good old Pavel, thought Stepan, don't worry about him! If he were drowning his last words would be, "Don't worry about me, I'll get along. . . ."

They entered the building in which the exam was being held, and as they walked along the hall they began to hear the buzz of voices of students waiting their turns outside the exam room. As they approached the group the door opened, and a plain-looking girl of about twenty years came quietly out. It was Ludmilla Liubov.

Everyone crowded about her. "What did you get, Ludmilla? How was it?"

She pressed her lips tightly together, trying to keep the quaver out of her voice, and murmured, "Two." She ran off down the hall followed by the sympathetic assurances of her friends.

Professor Gorovin had followed her out. He stood watching the students a few seconds. "Well," he asked, "who'll be next?" He looked around. "Aha, Citizen Gladkov. I'm sure you're not afraid to answer a few questions on Russian literature!"

Gladkov glared at the professor and detached himself from the group, while a murmuring started up among the students.

"Boy, old Gorovin has his nerve," whispered Pavel.

"Why, what's the matter?" Stepan whispered back.

"Didn't you hear? At yesterday's Komsomol meeting Gladkov

accused old Gorovin of formalism in teaching the Russian classics. . . ."

"Why, the little son of a bitch!"

Pavel looked at Stepan with one eyebrow cocked: "My, my, Stepanush, is that a quotation from Pushkin?   I don't recognize it."

Stepan blushed and asked: "But why would he do such a thing? Alexei Alexeievitch has been teaching Russian literature for thirty years.   Why should this suddenly be 'formalism'?"

"Hell, boy, you know that Gladkov.   He has to be a two-hundred percenter in everything.   Confidentially," he continued in a mock stage whisper so that the entire group could hear him, "I believe that Comrade Gladkov's concern with deviationism in the presentation of nineteenth century literature stems not so much from political zealousness as from a certain deficiency in intellect that makes the memorization of facts concerning various authors now dead a distasteful procedure.   Not, of course, that deviationism should not be pursued with vigor on all fronts."

The students snickered.   They could count on Pavel never to take anything too seriously.   It was always amusing to hear him slip with no hesitation from his usually slangy speech into the official jargonese.

An intense-looking thin blonde girl was passing along the corridor.   Spying Stepan and Pavel, she stopped to talk.

Stepan greeted her.   "Hello, Nina."

"Hello, Stepan.   Hello, Pavel."

"Hi," answered Pavel.   "Say, what are you and Stepan doing this evening?"

"I'm conducting a series of lectures on world proletarian literature at the Kaganovich works.   And Stepan is going to deliver the lecture tonight on the role of Jack London in the development of American proletarian literature."

Pavel nudged Stepan with his elbow, "Now, Stepan, old fellow, how does this happen?   Here I try for three years to get you interested in social work, and I get no place.   All Nina Ivanovna has to do is bend her little finger so, and you are up in front of a bunch of workers giving lectures."

Nina stamped her foot.   "Pavel, this is no joking matter."

"Okay, Nina, okay," he answered quickly. "I respect your status as an activist of the first order. Look, Vera and I are going to a movie. But afterwards we're going to a party at Anna Trudovna's. She wanted to know if you and Stepan could come over."

Stepan and Nina looked at each other. She nodded her head slightly, and he said to Pavel, "Fine, I guess we can get there about nine-thirty."

The door of the examination room had opened again.

Gladkov stamped through the group. His face was clouded over, and he refused to answer any of their queries.

Pavel uttered a sharp, "Phew! Guess I was right."

The professor looked around the group.

Someone pushed Pavel forward, saying, "Go ahead, hero!"

Pavel suddenly became sober, and walked into the examination room.

The other students continued their chatter, arguing over interpretations of various works, checking dates, asking advice. Stepan and Nina stood off by themselves discussing the lecture he was to give that evening. Finally she announced that she had to go on to her class in counterpoint and departed. Soon the door swung open and Pavel appeared, shaking hands with Professor Gorovin, looking jaunty as ever. As he turned his back to the professor, he flashed his right hand to the group with four fingers raised, rolled his eyes up at the ceiling, and let his knees go limp in a gesture conveying a tremendous feeling of relief.

Stepan passed him on the way in, and Pavel whispered, "Phew, was that close! Hurry up, I'll wait for you."

Stepan followed the professor into the dimly lit auditorium. A girl student who had preceded him into the room was sitting, trying to organize her thoughts. Professor Gorovin beckoned her over to the examination desk.

Stepan reached into the question box and pulled out the first slip his fingers touched. He quickly ran his eyes over the three questions and then walked over to a chair to sit and wait his turn. He swiftly outlined the answers he would give to each question.

The girl finished, and Stepan walked over to the desk and sat down without waiting to be called.

Professor Gorovin smiled up at him: "How are you this morning, Stepan Ivanovitch?" he said pleasantly.

"Very fine, Alexei Alexeievitch. Here are my questions."

The examination went quickly and pleasantly. The questions were all on topics which he and Professor Gorovin had discussed many times together. Stepan, the professor's favorite among the older students, had spent many evenings at the professor's apartment conversing informally. There was little doubt from the beginning that Stepan would perform well. When he finished the third question, Professor Gorovin smiled broadly and said, "Very good, Stepan Ivanovitch. You get a five."

The students congratulated him warmly, although they too had expected this result.

Pavel caught him by the sleeve and pulled him out of the group. They started to walk back to the dormitory.

"Boy," breathed Pavel, "did I ever scrape out of that one. Look, I get these three questions: 'Pushkin and his part in the Decembrist Revolt,' 'Gorky's *Foma Gordeev*,' and 'Compare Turgenev's heroes in *Fathers and Sons* and *Smoke*.' Pushkin I know something about, mainly what you taught me on the way over. Gorky I've got cold because I just read a long criticism in *Russkaya Kniga*. But—Turgenev! I didn't know a thing. Boy, I could see next year's stipend flying out the window, or maybe I should say being buried by Turgenev's heroes. I figured the only thing that was going to save me was to get him to concentrate on the second question. So, I started in like a ball of fire on Pushkin. He figures I know that cold and shuts me off and asks me to try the second question. So I begin to fumble and act like I don't know what to say. So he dives right in, figuring he's got my weak spot, and begins asking me a lot of detailed questions. Well, bit by bit I loosen up and give him a whole barrel of stuff on Gorky. By this time we've spent almost all the time on the first two questions, and he's so pleased with what I do on the second one that he waives the third one entirely. Phew! I get a four."

"That's swell," said Stepan, "but poor Ludmilla Liubov! I'm afraid the two she got means that she'll lose her stipend. Even if she keeps doing odd jobs to support herself, I don't think her family can help her enough to get her through."

"Yeh, that's tough," commented Pavel.

They walked on in silence, but Stepan kept thinking of Ludmilla. "You know, we had a girl in our village before the war just like Ludmilla—a girl named Aglaya Serovyan. She came back to the village because her stipend had been stopped by the edict of 1940, when Stalin said conditions were good enough for Soviet families to support the education of their children. Aglaya wasn't smart enough to get top grades and earn a stipend, and her mother had five younger kids to support. Aglaya tried working on the kolkhoz, but she couldn't give up her dream of going to school. The last I heard, she went to Kiev, where she was washing dishes in a cafeteria, trying to save up enough money to go back to school. I never heard of her after the war."

"Good God, Stepanush, if you will permit me a quotation from *Eugene Onegin:* 'What—another eclogue, Lensky?' Let's see, what would it be? Aha, 'Ode to Aglaya Serovyan on the day of her departure from the kolkhoz forever.' Boy, you better snap out of it. That poetry you read and write must be rotting your brain. Can't you find something more cheerful to talk about? How are you and Nina getting along? I should think she'd get some of that nonsense out of you."

Stepan both felt and looked sheepish. "Oh, we get along all right."

"I guess she's good for you—a little too serious for me though. I went around with a dish like that for a while. Wonderful figure, nice face. She wouldn't wear lipstick, and wore the most serious damned clothes you ever saw. Always talking like a *Pravda* editorial. I gave up on her after a while.

"I remember one night after a concert we walked through the Park of Culture and Rest," Pavel continued. "Just to keep the conversation going I kept yatching away with her about problems of postwar economic reconstruction, and American attempts to encircle our Socialist Fatherland. Well, we get to this park bench in a nice dark spot and I suggest we sit down and talk a while. Boy, would you believe it, that's just what we did. Talk! Christ, if I had wanted to talk I wouldn't want to do it on a park bench with a dish like that. Every time I put my arm around her she would say, 'Don't, Pavel, I'm trying to think!' Then she'd come up with another goddamned statistic. Uh, uh! That's not for me.

"Boy, I learned my lesson. Stay away from the serious ones, Pavel. That's what I told myself. If you really want to be sure of a good time, stay away from the students altogether. Get a working girl. Less complication. They know what they want and no fooling around about it. Did I ever tell you about the girl I picked up while I was still in Moscow during the war?"

Yes, he had told Stepan, but he would tell it again anyway. There was no point in trying to keep him off his favorite topic. . . .

"Well, I'm riding the streetcar one day, and I see this cute deal of a conductor. I start kidding her about this and that, and the first thing you know I got a date with her and one with her girl friend for my buddy. We pick them up, go to a movie, and return with them to their dormitory. So they sneak us right into the dormitory and into bed with 'em. None of your sticky socialist morality for them."

"I guess I just don't know my way around like you do, Pavel." Stepan was embarrassed as always at this turn of conversation. Apparently he was too shy, or maybe too serious. Try as he would, he was uncomfortable with the sort of girls Pavel favored. He didn't know what to talk about, and he was afraid he bored them. He often wished that Nina were a little more affectionate. Even in her seriousness she was different from him and more like Pavel. They both kept scolding him for being so dreamy and contemplative. . . . Well, he must get going and do some studying. He turned to Pavel. "Look, I have to drop in at the library," he said. "I'll see you tonight at the party."

Stepan spent the rest of the day in the library brushing up for the other exams which were coming up that week. At seven o'clock he met Nina at the metro stop. As he approached the stairs to the station he was greeted by Nina's crisp voice: "Well, I'm glad to see you're on time."

They took the metro to one of the Moscow industrial districts. Nina guided him through several blocks of the city to the gate of the plant, and from there to the plant auditorium. The workingmen were assembled, sitting about in ragged clothes and chatting with each other. The meeting was called to order. Nina made a few general remarks which tied Jack London into the previous lectures and related him to Charles Dickens of England as one of the great figures in Western proletarian literature. She then introduced Stepan.

Stepan talked for an hour. He began with a brief biography, outlining Jack London's history as a worker, his self-education, his difficulties in getting his work published, his own growing proletarian consciousness, and finally his impact on later Western proletarian writers. Stepan delivered his talk in a rather serious manner and somewhat nervously. The workingmen sat passively without moving, and a considerable number dropped off to sleep, which made him even more nervous. When he concluded, they applauded politely.

Nina asked if there were any questions. A few persons asked questions, mainly with a political slant. "Was the Wall Street monopoly successful in the present historical period in suppressing the publication of London's proletarian novels?" "Could you tell us more about the conditions of the English working class which awakened London to proletarian consciousness?" From their questions, their manner, and their somewhat better clothing, Stepan concluded that those who asked them were probably members of the plant's Party cell. The main body of workers remained apathetic and left hurriedly when the meeting ended.

As it was only nine o'clock, Stepan suggested that they take the metro part of the way and then walk the remainder of the distance to the party. This would permit them to stroll more than a mile along the Moscow river, as it was a clear, warm, spring night.

As soon as they were seated in the metro Nina began correcting his lecture manner. "The content was very good in general, Stepan, but you did not relate it sufficiently to contemporary conditions. In that way it was too formalistic. Remember that when you are talking to workingmen you must be more concrete. Don't just talk about social forces. Tell them about the workers and their families, how they were starving, and how the capitalist police beat them up when they protested."

"But, Nina, does it make any difference? Are those workers really interested in literature? You saw them sleeping just as well as I did. They're all tired out, and I'll bet that they would rather be home in bed."

"That's not the point, Stepan. I'm sure many of them would rather be home sleeping or drinking vodka. But it is the task of the Party and our task as members of the Komsomol to raise their level of literacy. Our policy is not like that of the exploiting classes of the capitalist countries—to surfeit the masses with pornographic literature and appeal only to their lowest motives. It is true that a certain amount of coercion is required to enforce attendance at these meetings, but the workers must be made more conscious of their role in society."

By this time they had come to their stop, and they continued the argument climbing up the stairs of the metro station out into the clear evening air.

"Nina, I would understand that better if the meetings weren't so exclusively political. I would like very much to develop the aesthetic sense of the workers. I could read them a poem about our beautiful city of Moscow."

"Stepan, sometimes I just don't understand you. You don't sound like a man of peasant background at all. You sound more like the offspring of the decadent Tzarist intelligentsia. I declare, such talk!"

"No, Nina. When I lived back in the village there were only a few dozen mud huts, but I used to dream about Moscow. It was like one of the fairy tales my mother used to tell me. Moscow was as unreal as the fairy tales. Even now when I look at the river and the Kremlin it still seems enchanted—so beautiful, so big, so full of strange life. I would like to teach the workers to see beauty as I see it."

"Really, Stepan, you do talk nonsense much of the time. Of course, Moscow is a beautiful city. But it's no fairyland. It is work that created it, and work alone."

"But, Nina, how can you take so cold an attitude toward aesthetics? Don't you find any enchantment in your music? How do you feel when you listen to Beethoven's *Eroica?* Don't you feel an upsurge of nobility, of some strange power, the ability to surpass yourself and make your dreams become real?"

"Stepan, you miss the point again. Of course, Beethoven's *Eroica* is great, but it is great precisely because he rejected his original intention to dedicate it to Napoleon, a tyrant who didn't respect the rights of the proletariat. The *Eroica* is great because it was created for the people. Music like everything else is for the people. They alone give everything value. Life has no other definition but people."

"But, Nina, it's not the people who create. That's an abstraction. It's one man who creates. Beethoven was not a mass of people. He was one man, with one brain, one soul. The very act of creation is something that distinguishes you from the masses."

"Stepan, why must you see everything in so complicated a way? Life is clear, and my goal is clear. I know what I'm supposed to do, and I do it. But you have to complicate *everything*."

"I'm not trying to complicate everything, Nina. I am only trying to find my own goal in life."

"Your what?"

"My goal in life. How can I judge that I am doing what I am supposed to do?"

"Judge? You don't have to. Your task is set out for you. To do your duty, that is it. That's your goal. You just obey, you—" Then, suddenly jerking her head, she exclaimed, "Oh, Stepan, this is absurd! Goal of life, indeed! That's something philosophers of a bygone age worried about. You can't fritter your life away in contemplation. It's like a childhood disease. If you're healthy you get over it by the time you're fourteen or fifteen. There's no such thing as *one* goal of life. There's only life, and the daily goal, or duty, of doing what you're supposed to do. . . ."

They were silent for a moment. Nina slipped her hand into his and swung it as they walked along. Finally she broke the silence again. "Look, Stepan, I don't like '*grands mots*' as the French say. Let's enjoy the party at Anna's. Come on, we're almost there."

He shrugged his shoulders. "All right."

When they arrived, the party was in full swing. There were about six couples, and the little white-washed room was so crowded that they could hardly move about. Pavel was standing with one arm around Vera, a buxom blonde girl, and he flourished a glass of vodka. They were singing Komsomol and revolutionary songs with great vigor.

Anna greeted them warmly at the door.

Pavel came over with a half-filled bottle of vodka and the two glasses. "Come on, Stepanush, you and Nina have to take a penalty drink to catch up. You're late."

Nina looked a little sternly at Pavel. "Better go easy, Pavel, or you'll be in no condition for the volunteer work brigade tomorrow morning."

Pavel grinned. "Don't worry about me, Nina. I'm on the committee. I'm the guy who told the volunteers that they were going to volunteer. Stepan and I will be there on time, and fit to dig ditches with the best of 'em."

Nina and Stepan had a drink "bottoms up."

The boy who was playing the accordion signaled to Nina, and she picked her way through the crowd, took the accordion, and began to play "Stenka Razin." Her voice came through the chorus of other voices a trifle strident in tone but clear and beautifully pitched.

Pavel pulled Stepan aside. "That swine Gladkov was here for a while, drinking up all the liquor," he said. "He's mad as hell. Gorovin gave him a one this morning. He says he's going to press the charges of formalism at the next Komsomol meeting. He was trying to get signatures on a petition to remove Gorovin, but nobody here would sign. I'm sure he'll get some bastards to sign it, though. It looks as if it might be a nasty mess."

Stepan's face flushed. "To hell with him. I'll tell just what I think of him at the meeting."

"You'd better be careful, Stepanush. You know that you've been awfully close to old Gorovin, and you could get in trouble too. I'm sure this character is working with the secret section. I shadowed him one time and saw him go into the local MGB office. The son of a bitch, he was trying to make a provocation here this evening. He started telling political anecdotes to see if he could smoke somebody out to tell more. I gave him a lecture on political morality. You should have seen Vera. She almost split her sides trying to keep from laughing when I started to lay him out for furnishing weapons to the enemies of socialism.

"Say, one of his stories was pretty good. I never heard it before. It seems that the hares in Poland near the border had been noticing a lot of strange hares around their territory for a while.

They began to suspect that the strangers were coming from our beloved Socialist Fatherland. So they sent a delegation to watch the border, and sure enough the first thing they saw was a hare coming over from the Soviet side running like his pants were on fire. They stopped him and asked him what the trouble was. He looked at them sort of surprised and asked: 'Didn't you hear? The Bolsheviks are castrating all the camels.' So one of the Polish hares said to him, 'Sure, but you're a hare, not a camel. What are you worried about?' The Russian hare said: 'Okay, I know I'm a hare, and you know I'm a hare. But those damned Bolsheviks. They'll castrate you first and ask you afterward.' "

Vera heard them laughing, and came over to pull Pavel into the circle of singers. "Come on, Pavlush," she giggled, pulling his arm around her waist. "Don't you like me any more?"

Nina and Stepan stayed only until about eleven o'clock. Nina didn't approve of carousing, and she wanted to be rested for the work the next day.

Early the next morning Stepan woke and shook Pavel, who was sleeping soundly without having removed his pants and socks from the night before. Pavel groaned as he got to his feet. "Oh, boy. Volunteer digging of ditches for gas mains. Just what I need. Right in the middle of exams!"

Stepan wagged his finger under Pavel's nose. "You have no one to blame but yourself, hero of socialist labor. You're the one who put the pressure on me to go."

They reached the location at eight o'clock. Some of the students were getting shovels from a tool shed. Others were standing about talking quietly. Nobody seemed particularly eager to get to work. Vera was there ahead of them, looking very decorative as she rested against her shovel and fixed her hair. When she saw Pavel she dropped the shovel and ran to greet him.

Nina appeared shortly afterwards, walking along conversing earnestly with the Komsomol Secretary. As the students saw him, they picked up their shovels and started to dig. Stepan and Nina shoveled silently and vigorously. Vera shoveled busily when an official was around, and directed idle comments at the other students in between times. Pavel spent most of his time walking up and down, giving orders to others, or conversing with the Komsomol Secretary and various Party officials who appeared on the scene.

When they stopped at noon, Stepan pulled a large piece of paper-wrapped bread from his pocket. Nina came over and offered him several radishes and an apple. They sat under a tree eating their lunch quietly.

Vera and Pavel walked by, their arms about each other's waist, with Pavel talking in a low pitched voice and Vera giggling.

Nina and Stepan followed them with their eyes.

Stepan commented. "They seem to get along very well together. They are very well matched."

Nina looked at him with raised eyebrows. "I agree with you, but I can't say that it is much of a compliment to either of them. I seriously think that the Komsomol should take some action on the general question of Pavel's morality. You know perfectly well how Irena Kavka became pregnant last year, and that she got an abortion from some doctor that Pavel's brother knew. That is no conduct for an activist in the Komsomol."

"Nina, I don't see how you can pass judgment on him that way. Neither you nor I nor the entire collective of the Komsomol has authority to judge a personal relationship between two people. No one else can know all the circumstances involved."

"You are completely wrong, Stepan. I have heard that argument before. But the Komsomol has both the right and the duty to be the monitor of the moral behavior of its members. As a body it is responsible for proper socialist feelings and actions in all moral matters."

"Well, as his friend I would certainly defend him," Stepan affirmed.

"As a friend you would be right. But as a citizen you would be wrong. This is typical of you, Stepan. You either get involved in high-flown abstractions like *a* goal of life, or you act on the basis of personal considerations. You must have more concern with your duties to the collective."

Mercifully for Stepan, work started up again, and he was saved from further moralizing by Nina.

Stepan and Pavel returned to their room after their "volunteer" work digging ditches. In the time before supper Pavel coached

Stepan for the exam on dialectical materialism which was coming up on the following day. As there was no text for the course, they had to rely mainly on Pavel's notes. In this instance, contrary to his usual cavalier approach to things, he had extremely full and well organized notes.

"Take these notes after supper," he told Stepan. "I won't need them. Bone up on 'em. Before the library closes you'd better skip over and reread Stalin's letter on linguistics. There's sure to be a question on that. It's a red-hot issue and they won't miss it. There's a good commentary on it in the last number of *Questions of Philosophy*. And look now, boy, when you write answers on this exam, don't get so damned abstract. Concrete and to the point—that's the deal. Stress the practical side of it. Throw in a couple of references to Josef Vissarionovich Stalin, our great and glorious leader. If you have any more time for reading, take another look at chapter eight of the *Short History of the Party*. . . . Well, good luck. I'm going to spend the evening learning some German. This stuff I know cold, but I'm rusty as hell on German."

Stepan passed the exam in dialectical materialism with a four. He got fives on all his other exams. Pavel did well also. He had all fives except for a four in Russian literature and in German. It seemed certain that they would both receive their stipends for the following year and be able to return to the Institute.

Nina and Stepan had their last exams on the same day. In celebration Stepan bought two tickets to a concert, a luxury that he could not often afford on his student's budget. He had thought at first of asking Pavel and Vera to come along, but decided that it would be more pleasant to spend an evening alone with Nina— if he could keep out of political arguments. They had known each other for several years, but had been going around together only for about three months. It seemed that Nina had used her entire time trying to remedy the deficiencies in his political training.

Tonight was different. The music swept politics and social problems out of her mind. She leaned over to Stepan in the midst of the piano concerto and whispered, "Some day, Stepan, I will be up there on that stage. I work so hard at it. I *must* succeed, I must." She slipped her hand into his and held it tightly, not in the comradely fashion with which she swung hands when they walked, but in a warm feminine manner. Stepan glanced at her face. It had lost its usual quality of intenseness and seemed to have become softer.

But once the concert was over, she was her old militant self. The matter of Gladkov came up again. Nina informed Stepan that Gladkov's charges would be heard at the Komsomol meeting the next day. She advised him to be present.

They said good-bye at her door, and he returned to the room. Pavel was still out. Stepan found a heel of bread on the window sill and munched it as he read for a while. Finally, when Pavel did not show up, he crawled into bed and went to sleep. He was disappointed not to see Pavel. It would have been good to discuss the next day's meeting with him. What could be done about Gladkov?

In the morning Pavel was sound asleep and refused to be roused. Stepan had certain details to take care of in connection with his summer studies and had to arrange for work during the vacation months. He left once more without talking to Pavel. The meeting was at two o'clock, and he got back just in time to find a seat in the hall next to Pavel; but the room was so crowded that there was no possibility of talking at length.

The meeting opened with the acceptance of two new members into the Komsomol.

Andrei Zumkov, a second year student, got up and gave a report on his past life. Pavel accompanied Zumkov's account with a series of caustic whispered comments.

"I have considered this step seriously for several years . . ." Zumkov said.

"You bet your life he has," whispered Pavel. "I've been on his tail for two years myself, trying to get him."

"A series of considerations intervened. . . ."

"You betcha. The first time he said he was politically unprepared. Then he lost the application blank. Then he couldn't find his fountain pen. Then he couldn't get anybody to recommend him. Phooey! I finally had to recommend him myself, and damned near had to fill out the blank and sign it for him."

Zumkov went on for fifteen minutes. The other candidate talked for twenty minutes. Finally they were voted in. Silly formalities, thought Stepan. Everybody knows these two were virtually forced in. . . .

Finally the moment came. Gladkov rose and made his charges. Professor A. A. Gorovin had taught Russian literature in exactly the same way, year after year, since the time of the Revolution. Obviously he was incapable or unwilling to learn from the experiences of the Revolution. First there was his blatant cosmopolitanism. Half of his course was devoted to the influence of Western writers on the Russian authors of the last century. Where in this course was there an adequate discussion of the effect of classical Russian writers, those pioneers on the forefront of progressive thought, on world literature? Next, Professor Gorovin takes a completely formal approach to his subject matter. There is no reference to contemporary problems. Russian literature is not taught from the point of view of the present day, but in an abstract fashion as though it had no relevance to the building of socialism or to the struggle for peace under conditions of capitalist encirclement.

Gladkov flourished a sheet of paper. "I have here a petition signed by seventy-five of our fellow students," he declared, "requesting that Professor Gorovin be removed from his post on the grounds that his teaching is politically inadequate."

Immediately frantic voices arose from various points in the hall. It was obvious that Gladkov's partisans had organized themselves as a claque. They began applauding Gladkov and shouting for the dismissal of Gorovin. A handful of students started to join them after a minute or so. This handful was composed almost exclusively of those drifters who tried to react as rapidly as possible to each developing trend. They thought it might be unsafe not to seem sufficiently enthusiastic in supporting Gladkov.

The secretary rapped for order. "Professor Gorovin has asked to speak. He has the floor."

Professor Gorovin, flushed and agitated, rose in the back of the hall and walked toward the platform. The claque began hissing and booing. The Secretary rapped for order again.

Gorovin began speaking hesitatingly, confusedly. Stepan writhed in sympathy with Gorovin. It was so embarrassing to see such a distinguished scholar in so humiliating a position, to hear his voice, which could deliver such crisp, incisive analyses of world trends in literature, shaking with anger, confusion, impotence. Gorovin could not come to grips with Gladkov's arguments. He spoke only of the glorious tradition of Russian and Soviet scholarship, of his long service in the Institute, of the immaturity of Gladkov and the students who made such charges. Even this he did poorly.

The claque took up their call again. "Dismiss him." "He's not a fit teacher." More and more students took up the cry as it looked as if the turn of events was going against Gorovin.

He stopped speaking and rushed down the aisle and out of the hall with tears running down his face.

Suddenly Stepan found himself on his feet, shouting above the din, demanding the floor. The Secretary recognized him.

He spoke so infrequently in meetings that the group fell into silence. The silence became deathly as his anger rang out through his first trembling words.

"This is a scandal." He could hear his voice pealing out as though it came from someone else. "Who would have dreamt that we would be confronted with the spectacle of Soviet youth being stampeded into demanding the dismissal of so distinguished a scholar as Professor Gorovin! Professor Gorovin is a man whose scholarship is respected throughout our country. He is even recognized throughout the world as one of the outstanding authorities on nineteenth century literature. If these baseless charges are to be accepted, our Institute will be robbed of one of its finest teachers, and a tremendous injustice will—"

By the end of his second sentence it had become clear to Gladkov's claque that Stepan was defending Gorovin. Now they started in to heckle him, to shout him down. There was a rising tide of voices. "Listen to the scholar talk!" "Sit down!" "You're the same kind." "Are we going to listen to such nonsense?" "Boo!" Then a concerted hissing and stamping began.

Stepan could no longer hear his own voice. He stood there bewildered and frightened. He felt Pavel jerk him back into his seat.

Gladkov arose again and was recognized.

"It is clear," said Gladkov, "what Comrade Gravinov's motives are. He has been very closely associated with both Professor Gorovin and the latter's point of view. Thus it is no accident that he alone should speak out in defense. I should further note that Comrade Gravinov has an additional ax to grind. His own grade record is enhanced by an unbroken string of fives given him by Professor Gorovin. He knows full well that if Professor Gorovin were dismissed, all of the grades which Professor Gorovin has given will be stricken from the record."

He looked about the hall with a smirk and sat down.

Stepan began to sense the danger of his own position. He did not regret having spoken up, but he realized that he had put himself in a position of jeopardy. This feeling was not at all relieved when Pavel whispered in a disgusted tone of voice, "Now you did it! Who the hell's going to get you out of this one, pal?"

Several short speeches were made attacking Gorovin and Stepan. Finally Pavel drew himself slowly to his feet and demanded the floor.

He began to speak slowly, sounding somewhat weary, as though he were having a distasteful task pushed off on him.

"Comrades, I will speak frankly," he said. "As you know, Comrade Stepan Gravinov is my roommate, and we have been friends for many years. Yet this in no way must blind me to the essential error he has made in his defense of Professor Gorovin. Comrade Gladkov has charged Professor Gorovin with formalism, with not relating his teaching of Russian literature to present day problems. But my friend here answers that Professor Gorovin is a distinguished scholar. That is not the issue."

His voice was getting more vibrant, and he spoke faster. Gladkov's supporters sent up scattered cheers.

"Let us speak to the point. What lies behind the charge of formalism? I think if we examine this point we will have something quite different to say from what our friend Comrade Gravinov has said."

There were more cheers.

"This does not mean that I necessarily agree with Comrade Gladkov. As a matter of fact, I think that as we examine this matter closely we will find that Comrade Gladkov is in very serious error. As our great leader Comrade Stalin has pointed out on many occasions, we must be extremely wary of those who are free in their use of 'leftist' slogans. This form of juvenile adventurism that we see expressed in Comrade Gladkov's charges is one of the most dangerous of the deviations which we must combat. If we were to take him seriously we would end up by ignoring our great literary heritage, developed by progressive Russian thinkers and writers of past centuries. In this period of conflict with the West we must guard on one hand against rootless cosmopolitanism which bows in admiration to the West, and against underestimation of our own historical heritage the dialectical elements of which are a source of strength in the present situation. Comrade Gladkov would like to have our history interpreted in terms of the present, but in so doing we must not reduce that history to meaningless phrases. We must understand it fully, richly, and not in the manner of the pet slogans of the leftist litterateurs of the RAPP period. I therefore move that Comrade Gladkov be found in error, and that he be instructed to attend better to his own political education."

A tremendous din arose. Gladkov's partisans booed and hissed, trying to offset some of the effect of Pavel's speech. Other students who had been silent to this point cheered him. Pavel leaned over to Stepan and under cover of the noise grunted, "That's the way to do it!"

Gladkov tried to get the floor, but the Secretary motioned toward the back of the hall and rapped for order.

A girl's voice came from the back of the room—strident, vibrant and live. It was Nina's.

"Comrades, I must agree with Comrade Zagordi. Comrade Gladkov's charges are a clear case of adventurous leftism. But I believe we must link these charges to the circumstances under which they are made. I would consider it in bad taste to raise such an issue if Comrade Gladkov had not already done so in connection with Comrade Gravinov's defense of Professor Gorovin. I join Comrade Zagordi again in my feeling that Comrade Gravinov is quite deficient in his defense. But, if Comrade Gladkov is to raise the question of motives, let us look into his own case. He has constantly lagged in his studies, particularly in literature. He has not kept his grade average up. He has never shown the diligence that is to be expected of a Komsomol member. It takes no great wisdom to see that he would benefit greatly by Professor Gorovin's dismissal, particularly in view of his own very poor performance on a recent examination." She paused. "Comrades," she continued, "you know me well, and you know the seriousness with which I hold our organization, the Komsomol. We cannot afford to let the morality of Soviet youth be perverted by such blatant opportunism as we see here this afternoon. The ability to mouth phrases cannot become a substitute for merit and truth. I move that Comrade Gladkov be officially censured for irresponsible and immoral conduct."

This time the hall was silent. The students waited for the Secretary to speak. He spoke quickly and to the point, endorsing the views of Nina and Pavel, but limiting the action against Gladkov to an unofficial rebuke.

Stepan was too much shaken by his own narrow escape to feel more than a sense of relief. Pavel took him by the arm and steered him through the crowd as the meeting broke up.

Stepan waited until they were clear of the others to speak. Before he had a chance to say anything, Vera came running up and took Pavel by the arm.

"Pavlushka, guess what!" she exclaimed. "I've been waiting for half an hour. Mother sent me a basket of fruit and some sausages. I just saw Nina, and we're all four going to have supper at my room."

Stepan saw that there was little chance of serious conversation as long as Vera was there. He walked along beside Pavel and Vera, listening to Vera chat away. They arrived at her room to find that Nina had preceded them. She had arranged the food on the table, and in the center stood a bottle of wine.

"My present," she announced, pointing to the bottle.

"Why, Nina!" quipped Pavel, "I didn't expect to find you contributing to the destruction of my morality."

"Oh, stop it, Pavel," she said half severely.

Vera went off down the hall to borrow a knife. Stepan looked at Nina and Pavel and said, "I must thank the two of you for saving Alexei Alexeievitch Gorovin this afternoon."

Pavel grimaced. "Look, wise guy!" he said. "As far as I'm concerned your friend Professor Gorovin can drown and old Pavel wouldn't risk his neck for him. Just don't get yourself in a position like that again. If you feel like Sir Galahad, at least learn how to handle such situations. Don't expect me to pull you out again. I could have gotten in just as much trouble as you if the decision went the wrong way. Whatever you do, learn how to take care of yourself if you get into one of those arguments. If a guy charges formalism, don't argue how pretty Pushkin's poetry is. Accuse him of left deviation. . . ."

Nina fixed her eye on him. "Pavel, who do you think was right? Is Gorovin a formalist?" she asked.

"Well," he shrugged his shoulders, "maybe! What difference does it make?"

She shook her head. "I must say that my remark about the ability to mouth phrases being no substitute for merit and truth applies to you as much as to Gladkov," she said.

Pavel looked at her and grinned. "Well, is he a formalist?"

"Yes, in my judgment, he is."

"Then, Nina, how does it happen that you spoke so eloquently in his defense?"

Nina blushed.

"There is no need to blush, Nina," Pavel added. "You were impelled by the same base motive I was; you couldn't let a comrade down. And I agree with you that even if he is a little naive at times he's a first-rate pal. I propose a toast to our pal." He poured four glasses of wine as Vera returned with a knife. "To Comrade Stepan—may he never need rescuing again."

Stepan blushed. Nina looked pleased, but slightly disapproving of Pavel's flipness. Vera said, "Bottoms up," and they drank the toast.

They had a round of bread and sausage, and then Stepan proposed another toast. "To Nina, who couldn't hide the warmness of her heart if she tried."

Nina raised her glass, smiled at Stepan, and turned to Pavel. "No," she said, "on the contrary, I propose a toast to all of us, because we can be each so different, and yet have something real within us that others can value."

Stepan smiled at her and said, "To that I can add only 'bottoms up.'"

Vera busied herself with more sandwiches, and sighed, "Oh, it's a shame that you're all going away for the summer. Are you going to take a vacation at the rest home in the country, Nina?"

"No," said Nina, "I decided not to ask for a pass. I would rather work for the month and earn a little extra money and hear some of the summer concerts."

"Same with me," added Stepan. "I have to get a little money."

Vera pouted and looked at Pavel. "Oh, Pavlushka, I suppose you're the only one who's leaving, and I'll be all alone."

Pavel grinned. "No, I'm staying too."

Vera giggled and put her head on his shoulder.

"How come, Pavel?" said Stepan. "I didn't know you were that hard up for money."

"Money? Hell no!" said Pavel. "But I know what I'd be in for in one of these so-called rest camps. There'll be three or four 'volunteer' brigades a week to go out and work in the kolkhozes. I'd rather be back with Vera than breaking my back in a cabbage patch." He slid his arm around Vera's waist and gave her a squeeze.

Stepan caught Nina's eye. They both looked over at Pavel and shrugged their shoulders in despair.

"I was taught," said Stepan, "that the new Soviet man should be like the mythical Greek hero, Antaeus, springing up with renewed strength from each contact with his mother earth. I suppose Pavel is the closest approximation of that I'll ever meet."

But Pavel and Vera were too engrossed in whispering to each other to pay attention.

Stepan reached for the wine bottle. "Would it be permissible, Nina, to propose a toast to the two of us?"

Nina nodded her head, smiling. Her glance was warm and friendly. . . .

The Woman Collective Farmer

Olga and her mother, Ekaterina, lay asleep on top of the stove on which they made their bed summer and winter. Olga slept soundly, but Ekaterina tossed and mumbled in her sleep—having another of her interminable dreams. In the morning she would bore Olga with the details. The baby began crying from his cradle hanging from the ceiling above Olga. She reached up half asleep and rocked the baby gently three or four times until he became quiet. Olga rolled her head away from the window through which the first grayness of dawn was showing and tried to catch a few moments more of sleep.

But the baby and the approaching dawn had awakened the chickens. The rooster began crowing at the top of his lungs, and the hens cackled and squawked in the far corner of the single room that made up the hut. Olga felt like throwing something at the chickens. Why, she grumbled to herself, can't you let me get my last few minutes of sleep? Well, she thought, I might as well get up. God knows I have enough to do before 7:00 o'clock.

Olga stumbled across the dirt floor, half tripping over one of the chickens on her way to the door. She flung it open and stood dragging in deep breaths of the night air. In a few hours the air would be heated by the hot August sun, but now it was cool and invigorating and helped to wake her up.

The baby was crying again. Olga rushed back into the hut.

The last harvest

They were more fortunate than many of their neighbors in having a steady supply of kerosene. Olga's brother was a tractor driver at the Machine Tractor Station and kept them supplied. With the lamp lit, Olga fixed a pacifier for the baby. She took a piece of rag from the shelf and grabbed a small mouthful of wheat with the other. She chewed the wheat until it was soft and moist, and then wrapped it in the rag. This she shoved in the baby's mouth, and the baby munched contentedly on it and stopped crying.

Olga prepared a thin gruel for breakfast. The sound of her activity and the smell of the gruel stirred Ekaterina from her sleep. She climbed stiffly off the stove and shuffled out of the hut mumbling to herself. Olga heard her relieving herself behind the hut. She reappeared through the door and sat down at the table. Olga shoved a bowl of gruel in front of her and she munched it with her toothless gums.

Olga sat down opposite her and began to eat.

"Mama," she said between spoonfuls, "look, you must start to dig our potatoes out today. We are behind on the harvest in the kolkhoz and I can't get any time to work on our plot."

Ekaterina kept eating and mumbling: "No time to work on our plot! Fine thing. Before the Bolsheviks came we had a good life. The saints have cursed them and cursed us all . . . took our land away. So now you have to work for them and our potatoes rot in the ground. . . . I dreamed last night that God set the old church on fire because the Bolsheviks made it into a clubhouse. Maybe he will strike them all dead. . . ."

Olga looked up from her bowl with irritation.

"Glory to God stop talking such nonsense, and quit whining about the past. Maybe you and Papa did have a good life before collectivization. But that's past and we're living now. We have to make out the best we can, so shut up! And keep your dreams to yourself or you'll have us all in trouble. God strike the Bolsheviks dead . . . fine chance!"

They had argued many times on variations of this theme. But as Olga had lost her patience with Ekaterina's clinging to the past and her hatred of the regime that had robbed her of her possessions and fought her religion, Olga had also lost her interest in the argument. It became a routine game in which each had a standard part. In truth Olga had little tolerance for her mother's attitudes. Possibly things were better in the Czar's time, or in Lenin's, or in some other land. But she was living here and now, and the problems of existence were too urgent to permit dreaming or reminiscence.

She looked across the table at Ekaterina. An old woman at fifty-five, toothless and feeble, slobbering away over a tasteless bowl of kasha. God! What childbearing, famine, and hard work could do to a human being! Only a month ago the brigadier insisted that Ekaterina was fit for occasional work on the kolkhoz. "A cracked dish," he said, "lasts for a century." Olga had pleaded and argued to get from the village doctor a statement that her mother was unfit for heavy labor. And today . . . she herself was urging Ekaterina to dig up their potatoes. Well, it was that or starve. If it hadn't rained last week, Olga would have dug them up herself.

She left her mother to work their plot only with the greatest of misgivings. There was no doubt but that the old lady was senile, and she was just as likely to pull up the potatoes as the weeds when the garden needed cultivating. Only God knew what she would do wrong in digging the potatoes out—still Olga had no choice.

Olga rose from the table, wiping the last traces of kasha from her lips with the edge of her skirt. "Remember to feed Seryozha, Mama. And take him out of the swaddling clothes at noon and in the late afternoon to let him play and develop his limbs."

Ekaterina came to life. "Don't tell me how to take care of the child. You would think that after twelve of my own I would know what to do."

Olga nodded silently. It was true. This was one thing with which Ekaterina could be trusted.

She picked up a heel of bread and started off across the fields for the assembly point. She looked up at the sun. Perhaps it was six-thirty. It was hard to tell. "Seven o'clock! The devil take 'em," she swore to herself. Olga had the peasant's antipathy to a schedule set by the alien device of a clock. Mama could complain all she wanted about losing her land, but what imp of Satan had thought up the idea of starting work at a given hour?

Olga bit at the heel of bread, tearing off a hunk in her mouth.

She walked rapidly through the field chewing at the bread, her bare feet crunching rhythmically against the wheat stubble. Across the horizon she saw figures approaching the assembly point from the next village. She looked up at the sun. The sky was clear and the sun bright. It would be a hot day. She took another bite of bread and strode on, her mind on the potatoes in her plot —they would need them to get through the winter and to feed the new pig—and Seryozha. Thank God, she thought, Ekaterina likes the child and takes good care of him. Olga remembered her mother's first reaction . . . it was a disgrace, the old lady shouted, to have an illegitimate child. But what did she expect? With twice as many women as men on the kolkhoz it wasn't easy to get married.

When she arrived at the assembly point the members of her brigade who came from the other village were already there. Several were standing about and talking. One or two were chewing on bread as she was. Igor Ivanov was ostentatiously eying the wrist watch he had picked off a German soldier during the war and looking over the fields for Evsey Grigorovich, the brigadier. "Five minutes to seven and I still can't see him!" Igor announced pompously. Igor was too dull-witted to work with the MTS or to get a job in the mill in town. He was the only young man who had been in the army who was still an ordinary field hand, but he tried to get a little importance by having the only watch in the brigade.

"Maybe Elyenka wouldn't let him get out of bed this morning!" one of the older women joked. "Elyenka is one of our best workers," the woman continued. "Only she earns her work days in bed instead of in the fields."

The field hands who heard her snickered. They all suspected that Evsey Grigorovich was fixing up the work records of Elyenka, his girl friend of the moment.

Olga laughed with the rest, and then said: "I don't mind Elyenka getting a few extra work days, but I wonder what our share will be this year."

Igor Ivanov addressed her: "My sister Irena Ivanovna, who is secretary to the Chairman of the kolkhoz . . ." (Everybody knew Irenka was secretary to the chairman, but this—like the wrist watch—made him feel important.) "She says that the harvest will be twenty percent over last year." He looked at their skeptical faces and shrugged his shoulders: "I just sold it for what I bought it."

"That's all very nice," answered Olga, "but it doesn't tell us what we'll get. I'll bet the government makes us deliver thirty percent more. Pfui, if the harvest is good they ask for more. If it's bad they ask for the same and take it out of our hides."

Several of the women nodded assent. But one of them whispered, "Here comes Evsey Grigorovich. You'd better shut up!"

Olga looked up and saw his stocky, big-boned figure striding toward them. He was accompanied by Elyenka, a girl of about twenty, tall, browned, with long strong legs and arms. She was not especially pretty, having a particularly large mouth and broad nose. But she had a pleasant and lively manner and managed to make herself attractive to the men. She made no secret of the fact that Evsey Grigorovich spent most of his nights in her hut.

Evsey looked over the group. "Everybody here? Good. Now listen to me, you lazy swine! You're going to work today, not like yesterday. We're way behind schedule. . . ." He continued to lecture for several minutes. The kolkhozniks listened without expression. It was a routine they went through daily with Evsey. He always told them they were behind schedule, whether they were or not. He operated by the primitive notion that nothing was to be lost by threats and curses—in fact they might produce a little more work. The kolkhozniks in turn closed their ears to his bawling out and were thankful occasionally that nothing worse befell them. "To blow hard like the north wind is not the same as sending us to Siberia," old Petya Fedorovitch would say.

Evsey finished his morning pep talk, and gave out the work assignments. Olga was assigned as "link leader" of four other women to follow the binder and stack the sheaves into piles. A wagon would come along later. The stacks of wheat would be loaded on the wagon by another crew and taken to the thresher. The other groups moved off to their tasks while Olga and her group waited for final instructions. Ivan gave them a special lecture: "You left over three acres of sheaves unstacked yesterday, you bitches. You'll have to make that up. And today you keep up with the binder or you'll sleep in the fields tonight. Now get going and don't give me excuses!"

The five women moved off silently to the portion of the field where the unstacked shocks lay.

Lizaveta Alexandrova, a plump, curvacious widow who had lost her husband during the war, walked alongside Olga. Lizaveta was particularly critical of Evsey. Kolya, the previous brigadier, had been her lover. When he went to the city to work she lost not only material favors he could bestow on her, but she found the young boys were not interested in a widow of thirty, and the men of her own age were almost all married and kept under strict surveillance by their wives. She grumbled about Evsey: "That silly ass! He's the worst brigadier on the kolkhoz. You'd think he was God himself now that he has a few people to tramp on. Will he let you off to work on your plot for a few hours? Not him! Will he lend you a horse when you need one? Not him!"

The other women let her grumble on. It was true that Evsey was particularly disagreeable. Kolya had been a more pleasant boss to work for. He had been sensitive to their needs and helped them out when he could.

"That Elyenka!" continued Lizaveta. "Did you see her this morning? Coming to work with Evsey! That little bitch hasn't any shame. It's all right with me if she gets plump as a pirovka from the food Evsey brings her for her whoring. But she doesn't have to advertise it!"

"Oh, shut up, Liza. You should talk. What's the matter, are you jealous?" two of the women shouted almost simultaneously. "Would you like to borrow my old man some night?" one of them asked.

Lizaveta giggled.

They stacked wheat sheaves for about thirty minutes before the MTS machines arrived in the field. The cutter and the binder began to attack the standing wheat, piling up new work for them before they had finished yesterday's sheaves. They moved faster and faster in their attempts not to fall behind.

Olga's body moved in a ceaseless rhythmic sequence of stepping, stooping, lifting, stacking. The sun was high and Olga was covered with sweat which rolled off her in continuous streams. For the first few hours they worked in silence. Even the garrulous Liza could not talk as she made every effort to catch up with the machines. Olga's world was composed of a few sensations . . . the ache of her back muscles as she lifted the wheat, the sting of sweat in her eyes, the taste of salt on her lips, the itch of bits of grain clinging to her moist arms and legs, the crunch and prickle of the stubble against her feet, and the bump of her body against the other women as they worked around the stacks. Gradually the sound of the machines and the occasional voices of the other kolkhozniks faded from her consciousness and she retreated into her thoughts as she labored.

She was occupied with mental arithmetic and planning. If she only knew what the kolkhozniks' share of the harvest would be! They wouldn't find out until the final accounting at the end of the year. And how would her labor days be counted? For field work like this you got the least amount of credits. It might take two days of work to earn one labor day. My God, she thought, if I could only have finished the seven-year school I could get a job in the office! But the family needed what she could earn in the fields and her mother had taken her out of school when she was ten. That was in '38, right after Papa was killed by a tractor. Now she needed the old lady. But Mama was getting old and deaf, and was very little help. As long as she could take care of the baby and help out with the plot! Everything depended on the plot. If the kolkhoz share was small or you got fined for some minor offense you could starve—not that things would ever be as bad as during and right after the war, she prayed. She had to take care of the plot and her chickens. Let's see, she calculated to herself, I have thirteen chickens and I have to pay the Raion twenty eggs a chicken—including the rooster, she smiled to herself. I'll have to pay the Raion the tax in eggs even if the chickens don't lay. I'd better make sure they're fed. I'll have to get some more wheat and corn for them. She began to plan how she might steal an extra bucket of grain that evening. Her musings were interrupted by somebody whispering, "Look who's coming. It looks like the Raion committee!"

Olga looked up from her work and saw Evsey and three other men approaching from a distance of about a quarter mile. As they came nearer the women could see that two of the men were dressed in suitcoats. There was no doubt that it was the Raion committee out to inspect the progress of the harvesting. The third man was Josef Vasilievitch, the Kolkhoz Chairman. Olga's group redoubled their efforts.

The two members of the Raion committee were questioning Evsey and Josef Vasilievitch. The women could not help noticing the difference in the way the two men answered their questions. Josef Vasilievitch was confident, direct, and to the point. Evsey was excessively deferential, and uneasy, trying hard to speak grammatically and to keep from swearing. He was explaining why his brigade was behind schedule, but the two Raion men seemed to be paying no attention. They talked to each other briefly and watched the women at work.

One of the Raion men suddenly said: "Look at this field! It's littered with loose stalks of wheat."

Olga looked out of the corner of her eye and saw that he was right. The field was dotted here and there with individual stalks of wheat which the binder had missed or which had fallen out of the sheaves. In their hurry to keep up with the binder they had no time to pick up such loose stalks.

"This is the people's bread," the man continued. "It is criminal to waste it. See to it that your people don't miss any more."

Evsey flushed and fumbled and tried to answer, but the words stuck in his throat. The kolkhoz chairman and the Raion men had already turned away and left before any words of explanation came to Evsey's lips. He turned on the women in his frustrated rage.

"You pigsnouts, you fat-bellied bitches," he sputtered. "You heard what the man said. You're wasting the people's bread. Pick up every one of those stalks. If I see another one on the ground, I'll fine you a dozen work days."

Olga and the younger women paid no attention to him. He always threatened to fine them for one thing or another, but he seldom had the courage to go through with his threat. However, Sonia Matveyevna, one of the older women in the group, spoke up. She straightened up and waddled over to Evsey, wiping her sweaty hands on her dress as she walked. She wagged her finger under Evsey's nose and said: "Evsey, you can take your twelve labor days, mix them with pig's dung, and eat them for breakfast. This morning you told us to keep up with the machine . . . yes? Now, you crazy idiot, you scream because we missed a few stalks. Pick 'em up yourself instead of standing here cursing."

Evsey flew into a fit of anger. "Don't talk back to me, you round-bellied pig. . . ."

Sonia Matveyevna wagged her finger more energetically. "Just because Josef Vasilievitch picked you for a brigadier you think you're God. When he spits in your eye you call it dew from heaven. You are a loafer now just like you always were. Now get out of here and see if you can't find Elyenka in some haystack. Don't bother us." She stood with her hands on her hips watching him until he got out of earshot and then went back to work.

Evsey walked away cursing and threatening Sonia Matveyevna over his shoulder. "Damn women," he mumbled, "their hair is long, but their wit is short." He began to run to catch up with the chairman and the Raion group.

Evsey felt very uneasy, and as he came within a few hundred feet of the Raion committee and Josef Vasilievitch he slowed to a walk, half hesitant to rejoin them. He was at home with the kolkhozniks, but with officials like these he had a feeling he didn't belong. They made him feel uncomfortable. Damn it all, he thought, I didn't want to be a brigadier anyway. All that happens is I get trouble from both sides.

If the cows get colic—who gets blamed, he thought—I do! If the field hands let a few stalks of wheat lie in the field—who gets blamed? I do!

And Josef sits in his office and makes me do his dirty work. When there's a meeting I have to go and tell everybody. And who do they curse at? Me! Josef should try to handle some of these bastards. Let him handle some of these old peasants like Sonia Matveyevna. They do what they damned well please and tell you to go to hell. Until Josef picked me out and made me brigadier, I was one of them. Now they treat me like dirt and blame me for everything the blasted officials make me do.

All I get out of it, he continued to himself, is a fixed number of labor days a month so I know better what my income will be, and a little power. And for that everybody wants me to do them favors . . . lend them a horse and a cart, give them time off to work on their plot or to go into town to sell something in the open market, or give them credit for a few extra days' work.

He thought of Elyenka and how she had come to ask a favor, to have the morning off to sow corn in her plot. He had begun to curse and berate her. But instead of becoming either angry or sullen she smiled and slipped her hand into his open shirt collar and around the back of his neck and said: "Now, Evsey, don't be cross. If I sow my corn and grain I will have enough to eat for myself and perhaps even cook for company now and then." He had wiggled uncomfortably as she continued: "Why don't you come around tonight after it gets too dark to work, and I'll show you how good I can cook." She stroked the back of his neck and pressed against him as she invited him over to her hut. His face flushed and he began to breathe excitedly. He would willingly have gone back to her hut with her there and then.

The Raion committee and Josef had stopped at a shed where several girls were sorting by hand wheat to be used for next year's sowing. As Evsey came close, the sound of their voices shook him from his reverie. One of the men, the new Raion committee Third Secretary, was complaining loudly about the way in which the sorting was being handled. Josef Vasilievitch was standing listening with his hands in his pockets, sucking pensively on his pipe, and nodding occasionally as though to acknowledge the justice of the Third Secretary's complaints. Evsey envied Josef's calmness in the face of the authorities. When the Third Secretary finished his harangue, Josef took his pipe from his mouth and replied: "Yes, Comrade Secretary, what you say is true enough and we shall do everything we can to improve the quality of the sorting. In the meantime I should like to call to your attention the fact that we requisitioned two automatic sorters last fall and they have not come through. Perhaps you could use your influence with the Ministry to get them to hurry up a little bit."

The Third Secretary protested that no excuses could be accepted, but Josef noticed with satisfaction that he had made a note about the sorters in his notebook. Josef didn't mind if they raved, as long as they did something to help out.

Now the other man, the First Secretary, began criticizing. The kolkhoz "Twentieth Anniversary of the October Revolution," he said, had gotten twice as much wheat per hectare as had Josef. Josef sucked again on his pipe and made a mental bet that the First Secretary would tell the chairman of the "Twentieth Anniversary" that Josef was getting twice as much yield as he was. Such tactics left Josef unperturbed. Things much worse than the rantings of an official could happen. He was a successful manager with an excellent production record and a good Party history. There was no need for him to get excited by the petty raving of the Raion Secretary.

"Well, Josef Vasilievitch," the First Secretary continued, "it doesn't look like you're in very good shape. You're behind schedule on the wheat threshing, and you still have the rye and barley to get in before you plow and seed your winter wheat." He paused for a moment. "You know what your wheat norm is for this year, don't you?"

Josef raised his eyebrows: "I thought it would be thirteen thousand, like last year's."

"Eighteen thousand bushels," the First Secretary answered.

"Eighteen thousand bushels!" Josef cried out. He had expected some increase because of the excellent crop, but this was more than he had counted on.

"Yes, eighteen thousand bushels," the First Secretary repeated. "The Oblast has raised the quota for the Raion by thirty-five percent, and your share of the increase is five thousand bushels."

Josef started to protest, but decided to keep quiet. This was something that would take looking into.

The Raion men indicated that their visit was at an end. They shook hands perfunctorily with Josef and Evsey and started across the fields toward the road on which their automobile was parked.

Josef turned to Evsey and said: "Evsey Grigorovich, I think we had better have a meeting of the brigadiers early this evening at my office . . . as soon as you knock off work in the fields. We'll have to do something to get the wheat harvested in a hurry. If we hit bad weather and can't get it all in, there won't be anything left over for us."

Evsey went on his way back to his brigade and Josef got on his horse which he had left at the sorting shed, and rode back to the office, a three-room, white-washed building. He went through the outer office into his own private office and closed the door behind him. He made two phone calls. This first was to the Second Secretary at the Raion Committee office. The Second Secretary, who was a friend of his, assured him that there was little if any possibility of getting the quota for wheat delivery lowered.

His second call was to Petya, the chairman of the neighboring stock-raising kolkhoz. Petya and he had often helped each other out in similar crises. They both acknowledged the need for a little initiative in dealing with fussy bureaucrats. "Petya," he asked, "do you have any empty silos? Good. Now I'll tell you what's up. The Raion Committee was around pestering me today. They want their wheat before it's out of the ground as usual, and they raised our quota five thousand bushels. If I know them, they'll be around as soon as we get their quota of wheat harvested and make us shift over to the rye and barley. You know the old argument— we can go back and get our share of the wheat as soon as we have filled the Raion's quota for rye and barley. Well, I don't want to take any chances of getting caught by bad weather before we get the kolkhoz's share of wheat in so I'll run a couple of truck-loads a night over to you and put it in your silos. We'll get it back in a month or so. . . . What? . . . Oh, you still have a few calves that don't show on the books! Why, you old scoundrel. Sure, sure we should be able to fix you up with a load or so for a couple of calves. Thanks a lot."

Josef hung the phone up with satisfaction. At least he would be able to assure the kolkhoz against bearing all the risk in the event that they lost some of the grain in the fields. Petya was a good fellow who would go along with Josef. Josef, in turn, would help Petya out occasionally. In the spring, for example, Petya drove a couple of dozen calves into Josef's woods so that they wouldn't be inventoried by the commission that inspected his kolkhoz. They both knew that they needed a little "reserve" here and there to help them over the tough spots. The MTS director had to be softened up occasionally with a side of beef or a few bushels of wheat. Even the Raion secretaries were not entirely above taking a "present" now and then. But Josef knew he had to take care of the kolkhozniks if the kolkhoz were to produce.

The bureaucrats were always trying to squeeze the last gram of grain out of the kolkhoznik. They couldn't see that a better fed and well-rested worker produced far more. A kopek plowed back into the kolkhoznik often yielded many rubles of return. Even as simple a thing as hot tea with lunch made a difference. . . .

He looked at his watch. It was one o'clock, almost time for the boys to take lunch to the field hands. He walked to the windows and looked out. There were hundreds of people and dozens of machines in the fields, some near and others so far that they were mere specks. In the distance, he saw a single speck approaching a small group. Aha, he said to himself, that may be Vanka delivering the lunches. He turned back to his desk pondering some way in which he could put the Raion First Secretary in his place . . . there must be some way of cutting him down to size, Josef thought.

Vanka was approaching Olga's group with the lunches. They had been working almost six hours under the hot sun. When they heard young Vanka shouting across the field, they stopped work immediately and sat themselves down in the shady side of the stacks of wheat while Vanka gave them their lunch of tea and black bread.

The very sight of food enlivened Liza and she asked Vanka, as he was pouring the tea, whether or not he had heard if they would have to sleep in the fields that night.

"Not tonight," he answered, "but I heard the bookkeeper say that he heard Josef Vasilievitch say that maybe tomorrow everybody would have to sleep in the fields and go back to work at daybreak. He's afraid we might get bad weather and lose the crop."

Liza looked coquettishly at Vanka. "How old are you, Vanka?" she asked. "You're getting to be quite a man. I don't know if it will be safe to sleep in the fields any more with you around."

Vanka blushed.

From behind another wheat stack came the voice of one of the other women. "I told you this morning, Liza, if you're hard up, you can borrow my old man. Leave the little boys alone."

Although Olga joined in the laughter, she sympathized with Vanka's embarrassment. He took up his large wooden pail full of tea and his bag of bread and hurried, red-eared, to the next group.

As link leader, Olga was supposed to get the group back to work as soon as possible after lunch. However, they all felt so relaxed from the food and tea and so tired from the morning's work that she let them sit in the shade for an extra fifteen minutes. They kept an eye open for Evsey and gossiped about the usual range of things—the harvest, a wedding in the village, someone's cow was sick, a villager had heard from a labor recruiter from the city that things were going badly with the new Five Year Plan, the cost of shoes was going up, there was a shipment of cloth coming into the store in town next week, the Raion Secretary had bawled out the chairman of the next farm for being too concerned with the welfare of the kolkhozniks and too little concerned with the welfare of the State. Gossip was the kolkhozniks' newspaper and they passed these tidbits of information from one to another with eagerness.

Reluctantly Olga called the lunch period to a close and they began again their hopeless chase of the binder—stepping, lifting, stacking, and stepping again to the next sheaf. The afternoon's work went much like the morning's except for the fact that the women had settled down to a somewhat more mechanical performance of their task. They were too tired to concentrate in the way they had earlier, and they worked a trifle more slowly and chatted back and forth a little more.

Toward the middle of the afternoon, they worked a portion of the field that lay close to the kolkhoz wood lot. Olga took pains to get herself as close to the woods as possible. Then she carefully missed sheaf after sheaf of wheat, being sure to leave those that were close into the trees and least likely to be noticed by Evsey if he came to check on their work.

As they worked away from the wood lot, she joined in the conversation again, hopeful that none of the other women had noticed her. She had no particular fear that any one of them would inform on her . . . but, the less people knew, the better.

Olga's group worked through until about 8:00, except for brief pauses. As the sun was beginning to go down, Evsey appeared again and told them that they could stop for the day. He instructed them to meet at the same place the next morning at 7:00

o'clock and be prepared to sleep overnight in the fields the following evening. Evsey said farewell to them with his usual barrage of curses, informing them that they would have to stop loafing and do a full day's work in the future.

Olga started for home. Sonia Matveyevna was going to visit her son who lived in Olga's village, so the two women walked off together.

Sonia was filled with opinions, information, and imprecations that filled up their time. She had a particularly juicy story to tell about Evsey.

"Olga," she began, "have you heard about Evsey and the potatoes?"

"No," replied Olga, "I haven't."

"Well," continued Sonia, "the first week he was a brigadier, before he was put over us, some of the kolkhozniks were digging up potatoes. One of the boys on the MTS thought he would play a joke on Evsey. He told him the women were planning to steal potatoes by tying them in one of their underskirts. He scared Evsey and told him how serious it was to take part in stealing socialist property. When the day was over, Evsey had all the women line up and patted their legs to make sure that they weren't getting away with any potatoes. The same MTS driver told one of his pals whose wife was working for Evsey that Evsey had worked up a trick for fooling around with all the women. This fellow came around to walk home with his wife just when Evsey was patting her legs and he gave Evsey a sock in the eye so it was black for days."

They were still laughing over this story when the machines from the MTS began streaming by on their way back to the barns. Fortunately Fedor, a tractor driver whom Olga knew well, came by and offered the two women a ride. They crowded up on the seat of the tractor and proceeded home at a rapid rate.

Fedor was about a year older than Olga and had been too young to serve in the army during the war. He was inducted into service immediately after the war's end and spent several years in the occupying forces in Germany. There he was taught a "specialty" —driving a truck. When he returned to the village a year ago, he went to work for the MTS driving a tractor. Fedor enjoyed the fact that there were many more women than men in the villages and it seemed unlikely that any girl was going to get him to settle down and get married very soon.

Olga was one of the girls he met at the dances in the kolkhoz clubhouse and exchanged pleasantries with in the fields. He did not regard her as particularly attractive, for indeed with her round, dumpy figure and plain face she wasn't. But she was pleasant and friendly. Fedor had never accompanied her home from any of the dances, but now as he looked at her snub nose silhouetted against the night and felt her pressed against him in the crowded seat of the truck, he made a mental note to do so after the next dance.

Fedor called across the seat to Sonia Matveyevna, "Mama Sonia, what do you think of our friend Olga here. Isn't she the prettiest girl in the village?" And he slipped his arm around Olga's waist, giving her a ludicrously exaggerated hug.

Olga giggled, but Sonia Matveyevna, who regarded machines with great respect and anxiety, pleaded with Fedor to drive the tractor with both hands.

Olga and Sonia Matveyevna got off at Olga's village while Fedor and the tractor continued on to the MTS barns down the road. Olga had enjoyed the ride, sitting next to Fedor and talking with him. Now the prospect of returning to her hut depressed her. It was dark. The moon had not yet risen, and she had to walk carefully over the field to her house. As careful as she was, she almost stepped on the chickens huddled outside the door. She cursed Ekaterina to herself. The old woman had forgotten to let the chickens in the house, and probably had forgotten to feed them too! She opened the door and looked in. Ekaterina was sleeping already on the stove, and the baby was swinging quietly from the beam. Olga stepped outside again to look at the garden. Thank God, the old woman had dug up a few potatoes at least. It was not as much as Olga had hoped for, but at least it was something.

She returned again to the house and made herself some supper. By this time, the baby was awake. She took him down and removed the swaddling rags, carefully unwrapping him from the endless sheath in which he was bound stiff as a board. He kicked and stretched himself in the joy of being able to move his limbs freely. Olga fed him and then played with him for a while. She looked at his strong, straight arms and legs and his long body, and thought fleetingly of his father who had left the village for the city before he ever knew Olga was pregnant. But she quickly put those thoughts out of her mind, swaddled the baby again, hung him back in his cradle, and returned to her household chores.

She finished her mending and washing of the baby's things by the light of a candle. She used the kerosene lantern sparingly. When this was completed, she went to a corner of the room behind the stove and removed a box which was standing there loaded with wood. Beneath the box was a hole about a meter deep which she had dug in the floor. From this hole she removed two large sacks, and placed the box back in place. It would soon be late enough so that most of the village would be asleep. Then Olga would return to the woods where she had left the shocks of wheat and retrieve the grain for herself.

After making sure that the baby was sleeping soundly, she hurried off across the fields with the bags tucked under her arms. She came to the place where she had dropped the shocks. Olga carefully pulled a half-dozen sheaves back into the woods and worked over them feverishly, stripping off as much wheat as she could with her hands. She succeeded in getting only about half the wheat off the stalks and got a good deal of straw along with it. It would be necessary to thresh the straw out when she got home. As she finished with each sheaf, she carried it about a hundred feet back into the woods and threw it into the stream that flowed by. By morning the sheaves would have been carried downstream and it would be impossible to tell from where they had come.

While Olga was busy stripping the wheat from the sheaves in the woods, Josef was bringing the meeting of brigadiers to a close. Evsey took his leave from the group and started off in the direction of Elyenka's hut. When he was out of sight of the others, he doubled back quickly to one of the kolkhoz storage buildings behind which he had secreted a bucket of grain at the end of the day in the fields.

Josef hurried over to the barns where the trucks were loading to take the wheat over to the stock-breeding kolkhoz. He had assigned four men whom he could trust implicitly to do the job, but he thought it best to go along with them so that there would be no hitch on the other end.

Olga finished stripping the sheaves and loaded both her bags. She walked to the edge of the woods and looked across the fields. She froze against a tree as she saw the figure of a man swinging across the field, skirting the edge of the woods. As it drew closer, she recognized it as Evsey, and saw that he was carrying a bucket. The weight of the bucket made him walk with a slight list. "Aha," she murmured, "he's taking a bucket of wheat to Elyenka."

Suddenly she heard a noise, the noise of truck engines. Evsey must have heard it too, because he stepped back into the shadow of the trees. The road came within a hundred yards of the woods at this point, and then cut in sharply a quarter of a mile below to cross the stream. Soon Olga saw two trucks speed by on the road and about a minute later heard them rumble across the bridge.

As Josef's trucks crossed the stream, he looked down at its waters shining in the moonlight. Suddenly he swore so violently that the driver almost lost control of the truck. "The bastards," Josef shouted, "look at those sheaves of wheat floating down the stream. Some son of a bitch got half the grain off of them and threw them in the water to hide the evidence. The lousy swine. It's bad enough to steal kolkhoz grain, but the pigs throw half of it away. I'll have to double the night guards from now on."

Evsey, hidden in the trees, grinned at the disappearing trucks. "Josef isn't fooling me," he chuckled. "So that's why he hurried off in the direction of the barns. I wonder where he's going with it? Well, that's his business." Evsey lifted his bucket of grain and continued on his way.

Olga waited until Evsey was out of sight and then picked her way back home, stopping frequently to rest under the weight of the two bags of wheat. By the time she reached the hut again, she was almost too exhausted to hide the wheat. But her body responded once more and she dumped the bags into the hold in the floor before she went to sleep next to Ekaterina on the stove.

The Woman Doctor

Nadezhda Ivanovna Popova arrived in the city fresh from the country—bright, eager, spurred by the dream of becoming a doctor who would be loved and respected by the people, who would return to the village to be a leader of the life of the community like the bearded patriarch who rode to her house on horseback when she was sick.

At first her fellow students, mainly city dwellers from families of the old intelligentsia, regarded her with amusement. They smiled at her lack of sophistication, at her peasant manner and speech. They were amused at her enthusiasm and overflowing energy. But what she lacked in sophistication, she made up in native ability and hard work, and so she soon won a favored place in the student body.

There were many different groups among the students. Some were young idealists like herself, bent on building a new system of social medicine by becoming the best possible doctors. Some were more politically-minded students who joined the Party and intended to become medical administrators. Others, mainly boys, could not get into technical schools because of lack of ability or a poor social background, and had entered the medical profession only because it offered the best opportunity for a reasonably satisfactory career and way of life. Despite these differences, all the students were to some degree caught up in the spirit of "progressive

ИСТОРИЯ БОЛЕЗНИ

Рис. А. БАЖЕНОВА

— Доктор наотрез отказался выдать мужу бюллетень, и он так расстроился, что даже заболел!

The History of an Illness.

—The doctor absolutely refused to give him a sick excuse, and he got so upset that he really took sick.

Soviet medicine," in the belief that a new and revolutionary approach to medical problems was being evolved which would improve the welfare of the people. They believed that this system was part of the new social and political order which was being built.

Nadezhda Ivanovna was among those most imbued with this hope. This was the time of the "brigade system," that comical arrangement whereby you studied and passed exams in a group. And there was Nadezhda, a regular "activist," urging, cajoling, helping her fellows with their work. She regarded the old and venerable professors with something of an amused tolerance. They were very fine specialists, she thought, but really relics of an antiquated social order and an outmoded system of medicine—while younger, more progressive instructors, some doctors and others Party officials, taught principles of public health and Marxism-Leninism. They were the prophets of the new order, of the Soviet system of medicine. And yet one small doubt clouded her mind—when she was alone out in the villages she might be willing to trade all the lectures on the organization of public health and on Marxism-Leninism for the opportunity to ask one simple question of these old specialists—one question that might save a life. . . .

Nadezhda Ivanovna's introduction into "Soviet reality" began just before graduation from medical school. She observed the maneuvers through which her fellow students attempted to get favored assignments. A boy with an uncle in the Commissariat of Health managed to remain in the city—contrary to practice which said that every young doctor should serve an apprenticeship in the villages. A girl friend who was married to a student of chemistry sought out friends and acquaintances who might know somebody in the Commissariat who might give her an assignment in Moscow, where her husband was going to do advanced work. A dunce who had joined the Party was lifted out of school before graduation to take an important administrative post in a new polyclinic.

As for herself, Nadezhda was eager to go into the villages. This, after all, was what she had been trained for.

Nizhnyi Simbirsk, her assignment read, a small village to the east of the Urals, a small village that had never had its own doctor. The village had been served since before the Revolution by a feldsher who handled most of the medical problems of this and several surrounding villages, referring only the most difficult cases to the doctor in the nearest large town.

She arrived in the village late on a summer afternoon, seated on a peasant's cart in which she had made the fifty-kilometer trip from the nearest rail town. The region did not yet boast a motor bus, but the young peasant who drove the cart told her with pride that they now had a Machine Tractor Station and that agriculture would soon be mechanized completely. The Village Soviet, he continued, had arranged for the construction of a new building to accommodate the expanded medical service. As they entered the village, he pointed it out to her—a small one-room hut.

The first few months were difficult. There was much that Ivan Fedorovich, the feldsher, could teach her about the actual practice of medicine, and she was eager to learn it. He, on his part, could see only the negative side of this green young doctor fresh from medical school. Several times she overheard him refer to her as "our lady friend from the Institute." What he taught her was not through a desire to be helpful, but indirectly through sarcastic comments, and by exposing her to the realities of Soviet life.

One morning a peasant showed up at Nadezhda's small office and asked for a slip excusing him from work on the kolkhoz for two days because of illness.

"What's wrong?" she asked.

He grumbled, "Nothing's wrong with me, I just want the slip. I want to go into town and sell some produce in the market."

She ushered him indignantly from the office, scolding him for presuming that she would aid him in evading his duties.

When she related this incident to the feldsher later in the day, instead of the vehement agreement which she anticipated, she was greeted with the surly comment, "Our job isn't to keep people from earning a living." Gradually she became aware that the doctor's job involved more than physical treatment. She was the official arbiter who decided whether or not a person worked or did not work. Her clinical thermometer was a sort of magic wand in the village. If its red line reached a certain point, you did not have to work; if she signed a slip, you could go home to bed. This precipitated the first political crisis in Nadezhda Popova's life.

An epidemic of influenza hit the village at harvest time. For two mornings she sent ten and then twelve patients home to bed. On the afternoon of the third day, as she rode back from visiting a neighboring village, the chairman of the kolkhoz ran out of his office to intercept her. He shouted up at her: "I sent those damned loafers back into the field. We have a harvest to get out, and I can't have twenty-two hands staying home to rest up. I thought you were a doctor! You let every faker in the village get away with murder. Why, I found Antonov out working on his own plot."

She reined in her horse and sat flourishing her medical kit in one hand while she waved the reins in the other until she almost frightened the horse into bolting.

"Look here, Trofim Andreevitch, I'm the doctor. If I say a man stays home, he stays home. When I saw Antonov this morning, he had a fever. He belongs home in bed. I can't stand over every muzhik in the village to keep him from working on his plot. Furthermore, tomorrow morning, I'm sending home everybody who belongs in bed. You're the collective farm chairman—I don't tell you how to harvest wheat—and you don't tell me who is sick and who isn't."

They argued back and forth for half an hour. Finally she rode off in a fury, with the chairman shouting down the road after her.

The next morning the line of patients was larger than usual. Half frightened by the prospect of a worse fight with Trofim Andreevitch, and realizing the urgency of the needs of the harvest, she was especially severe with the first few people. But there was no denying it. They were sick, very sick, and they belonged in bed. What good was it to harvest the grain if nobody would be alive to eat it? That morning she sent fifteen of the original twenty-two back to their huts, and an additional twenty more.

Before she was finished examining all those who were waiting for her, Trofim Andreevitch and the local Party chairman came striding along the road.

Nadezhda Popova saw them through the window of the hut. It was plain to her from the energetic way in which the chairman was waving his arms that she was the point of discussion. Sure enough, they stopped in front of the hut. The Party Secretary stepped inside the door. "Citizeness doctor, would you please step outside?" he demanded.

Her heart sank within her. This was the first time that she was ever involved in an "official" fracas. What would he say?

As she stepped out into the open, she saw the chairman stomping back and forth in a fury. "Show her the instructions, Semyon Semyonovitch," he shouted. "Show her the instructions."

The Party Secretary said ponderously: "I am given to understand that you are obstructing the work of the harvest. The task of building socialism in one country cannot be impeded by misguided bourgeois sentimentalism. Our comrade needs these people to bring in the—"

All of her caution and fear were forgotten. "Bring in the harvest, bring in the harvest—is that all you can think of? These people are sick, and I am a doctor. If I say they go home, they should go home."

The Party Secretary reddened, and he pulled out from his coat pocket a paper which he carefully unfolded before her.

"Without a doubt you do not realize the seriousness of your actions. I have here instructions from the regional Party Committee concerning the urgency of gathering the harvest at the earliest possible moment, and it specifies that no consideration shall interfere with this goal. If you continue in your obstructionist tactics, I must warn you that your behavior will be considered to be a counter-revolutionary act. There, read it for yourself."

She grabbed the paper and stared at it, caught between alternate waves of anger and fear, seeing only isolated phrases that seemed to jump out from the paper and beat against her throbbing breast—"utmost urgency" . . . "critical need to fulfill the plan for grain export" . . . "need for Party vigilance" . . . "diversionist attempt" . . . "counter-revolutionary sabotage" . . . "bourgeois humanitarian misconceptions" . . . "thoroughgoing

Bolshevik concern for the goals of the Plan" . . . "complete ruthlessness with the class enemies of the Socialist state . . ."

"I trust, citizeness, that you do not want to be personally responsible for the failure of the harvest. Remember the cord breaks where it is weakest, and we have a habit of discarding the weak pieces," he added, giving a menacing twist to the old proverb.

"Yes, yes . . ." and she went back to the hut, dosed most of the patients with aspirin, and sent only the two or three worst back to their huts.

When the last patient had left, she shut the door behind him, and broke into tears—tears of anger, despair, pity, futility. Was she a coward? Suppose she had resisted, would it have helped? Was she right? Could she or these poor sick peasants stand in the way of progress, of the needs of the country? Was their individual welfare more important than the whole program of socialization?

Such intrusions of politics into medicine became part of her everyday life, but they were by no means the most important part. Her day was dominated by children with measles and runny noses, pregnant women, men with cuts, bruises, broken bones, hurt less by pain than by the humiliation of being the victims of the strange new machinery that was being brought into the collective farm. Here she was in her medium. Gradually she and the feldsher mended their differences and united in their efforts to serve those who needed their aid. Helping and healing, bringing new citizens into the world—these duties filled her day and her heart, and gave purpose to life.

At the end of her third year she applied for a refresher course at her old Institute and was accepted.

She returned to the city with something of the feeling that she had when first she arrived from the country, struck by the activity, the noise, the differences in clothes and manner and speech. The first several times she spoke to someone she attended self-consciously to her own accent to make sure that she had not slipped back into village speech. But soon she felt at home again, with that somewhat warmer feeling of belonging to a place that comes from having once been away.

Old friendships were renewed. There was Alyosha who had gone into the Party and was now assistant director of a new clinic.

He had grown a little pompous, and now spoke earnestly of the importance of Party cadres in the development of the organization of Soviet medicine, of the need for increased political vigilance on the part of Soviet doctors. "We have to watch to see that every faker in the city doesn't come around trying to get out of work by pretending to be sick." He told proudly of the new system of work norms he had developed for the clinic. Nadezhda protested hotly: "Medicine isn't like a factory. You can't tell a doctor he has to treat so many patients an hour!"

"On the contrary," he would rejoin, "we must extend the principles of planning to all of Soviet life. How else can we make maximal use of our resources?"

These arguments would go on endlessly, filling in the intermissions of the concerts they attended, and sometimes carrying over into the performance to drown out the music.

Gradually these disagreements became the focus of their relationship. He began to berate her for being politically backward (she who had held the brigade together and helped him through his exams!); and she accused him of having lost his feelings of humanity (he, the sentimental student who had brought her the first flowers of the year from the street vendors). Their dates became less enjoyable, and gradually they stopped seeing each other.

She also renewed her friendship with Professor Petrovich. The Professor was a distinguished specialist in internal medicine, trained under the Czarist system. He had spent several years in western Europe in the early years of the NEP. It was something of an adventure to visit him. He remained an outspoken critic of the regime, voicing his opinions freely except on the most public of occasions. But his skill and training brought him political immunity and a standard of living that few men in the city enjoyed. He worked almost exclusively in the "closed" hospitals reserved for the top ranks of the Party and the NKVD. He was also one of the very small group of specialists who had a lucrative private practice.

"Look at this!" he would snort, shoving his hands deep into his coat pockets, jerking his head toward the various parts of the room, and pointing with the tip of his beard at the lamps, the sofa, the radio, and the phonograph. "Who else lives like this? I have my own automobile assigned to me. I have a dacha of my own. Five rooms in this apartment. Why? Because they need me. When the Secretary of the Obkom has a bellyache, I have to assure him that he doesn't have an ulcer before he dares take a teaspoon of bicarbonate of soda. For two consultations I get paid as much as an ordinary doctor does for a month's work in a clinic. I tell you, Nadezhda Ivanovna, become a specialist. Especially become a very learned specialist on something that the big shots are scared of dying from. You must realize the enormous privilege it is to be a non-Party person so highly respected? None of the big shots would trust themselves to the hands of a Party doctor; all he can do is make speeches, set norms, and push paper around. Our peasants say: 'A nightingale is not happy in a golden cage,' but few of us are nightingales. You too can live well."

Then she would argue on the other side, defending the way in which the regime had brought medicine to the people. "It is true that you get large fees from the big shots, Professor Petrovich. But you also work in the clinic. The working people can come to you free."

"Rubbish! Under the old system I did charity work, too."

"But now it isn't charity. It is the people's own system of medicine. They get medical care because their own state provides it. Besides, I don't see how you can talk like that! You are a doctor. A doctor does not work to help himself, but to help others."

He would smile gently, and say, "Yes, that is very true. Even under the Bolsheviks we can help people, and there are many more of us than there were. You are quite right. But—" and he would return to the attack—"look who goes into medicine these days, and look how they are treated. The best become engineers, and it's the engineers who get the best pay and have the greatest respect. But what kind of an order of things is there where the man who repairs machines gets more respect and better pay than the man who repairs human beings? Answer me that!"

On such points she would get confused, answer in trite formulae, never quite sure that she was right. She remained proud of the system of socialized medicine, but, good as they were, Soviet doctors were not the cream of Soviet manpower. This was why so many, more than half of the doctors, were women, and why a man with a suspicious social background could get into a medical school although he couldn't get into an engineering school or a scientific institute. The pay of a doctor was scarcely more than that of a common worker. Her colleagues all held down two full-time jobs. Despite the fact that they worked twelve hours a day, they were still shabbily dressed, poorly fed, and ill-housed.

But for all of his disturbing political arguments, the Professor was nevertheless an urbane, cultured man, amusing and interesting to talk to, and Nadezhda Ivanovna continued to visit him and enjoy his conversation and food, and listen with him to the music of western Europe on his radio and gramophone.

With his help she obtained a post in one of the most modern of the clinics in the city and began preparing herself for specialization in obstetrics and gynecology. She found she had more to learn than medical principles. Work in a big city clinic was different in many ways from practice in the village. There were the infernal norms. She was under constant pressure to turn out a prescribed number of patients an hour. Appointments were made on that basis, and she had to take care of the patients. Reluctantly she accepted the fact that one could not give every patient the attention she deserved. One had to rush through the simple cases to have time for the difficult ones.

There were big advantages, though. Equipment in the clinic was better than she had dreamed of in the village. Drugs were seldom in short supply. And there were specialists in every field who could be called on for consultation in difficult cases.

In big city clinics one had to attend meetings regularly, some professional, most of them political. She had almost forgotten what it was like to be a member of a working collective. Here she was back in the midst of the old slogans and exhortations to which she had responded so eagerly in school, but now they tended to be boring intrusions on a busy day.

The routine was stricter, and she was more accountable for her work. She was accountable, she discovered, not only to her superiors, but to the patients. A patient could lodge a formal complaint if he was dissatisfied, and the responsible administrators had to review it unless it was too obviously the product of an unbalanced mind. Periodically, Nadezhda had to sit on a medical board to review complaints that had been made by patients against one or the other of the doctors on the staff of the clinic.

The first of these cases made a vivid impression on her. A Party Secretary had been referred for consultation to a distinguished urologist. The urologist had given a diagnosis of syphilis. The Party Secretary charged the doctor with having infected him with the disease by using a contaminated hypodermic. The charge was obviously ridiculous; but considering the seriousness of the offense which was alleged, and the importance of the person who made it, the ritual of an investigation had to be followed out. The urologist, a specialist of impeccable reputation, defended himself anxiously. He recited the details of the case and gave a step-by-step account of the procedures and precautions which he and his nurse used for sterilization. As he told his story and answered the questions which were directed at him by the members of the board, he watched searchingly the faces of his colleagues for some cue as to how they would act. The verdict was what had been expected as a matter of course—that he was blameless. But the fact that one was cleared of such charges did not appreciably lessen the feeling of danger and the indignity of having to answer the complaints of any peevish patient who wanted to file charges.

Relations with patients were much more complicated than they had been in the village. Throughout Soviet society the doctor was caught between the needs of the patient and the needs of the State. But in the city these pressures became more acute. Supervision and control over the doctor were much more detailed and strict, and the needs and problems of the patients were more urgent.

Part of this she learned from her own experience, and part from friends who were working in other branches of medicine. When she had returned to the city, she had been faced with the chronic problem of city dwellers—where to live? A friend of a friend was a woman physician, unmarried, who worked in the health organization of a factory. She, Vera Dorofeovna, had a small room which she was willing to share, and Nadezhda Popova moved in with her. Evenings when they were home together they matched experiences, and Nadezhda Popova acquired a better perspective on the functioning of the medical system in industry. She learned that under the vaunted banner of "Socialist competition" physicians were urged to keep to a minimum the number of sickness certificates excusing workers from the job, and that quotas were set for the number of persons who could be excused.

Vera Dorofeovna was especially angry one night. She had been called into the office of the Chief Physician to explain why she had issued twenty percent more excuses from work than she had in the previous month. ·"Because more people were sick," she told Nadezhda, "but do you think he would listen! Imagine the situation we are in. The wife of the factory director is one of the doctors. She keeps sending the workers back to the job until their condition is aggravated and they come to someone else who eventually has to excuse them from work. And now she's held up as an example to us!"

But there were other pressures, from the workers, on Vera. These were days of food shortages, and workers would come to her begging to be excused from work for a day so that they might go into the country and try to buy food for the family. Occasionally she would return home in the evening extremely depressed. "What can you do?" she would say. "What can you do? Goodness knows, I would like to help them. One of the women came to me today and cried until I thought my heart would break. She has two children, her husband is dead, and she has no babushka to look after the kids. She wanted to get a day off to trade the last of her husband's clothes for some potatoes. But I didn't dare let her off. Suppose someone found out? Suppose this was just a provocation?"

More sophisticated workers would not approach the doctor so openly, but might feign the symptoms of disease. "You know," Vera commented, "it's getting to the point that our socialist state is developing a very enlightened and educated citizenry. The workers in our factory must stay up nights learning how to feign a disease. There isn't one worker in ten who can't produce a fever or a rash on demand with the aid of ordinary household materials. Seriously, it is a very real problem. Here I am, a doctor trying to help them, and I can't even trust the symptoms I see, let alone the ones they report to me. I have to be a better detective than the chief of the Spetsotdel himself."

Nadezhda was not long spared these experiences. She had begun work in the clinic in 1936, just before the regime reversed its policy and made abortions illegal. One day she was performing abortions in line with a policy of social enlightenment that said no woman should have a baby unless she wanted it, and the next day it was a crime to perform such an operation except under conditions of medical necessity. True, there had been excesses, women who did not want children, who regarded them as an interference with their own pleasures—women who were completely irresponsible in their attitudes. But now there were excesses in the other direction, women who would have wanted children but whose circumstances made this impossible. What might have been a joy in their lives became a threat of disaster. How was a doctor to react to such drastic changes in policy?

At first they came in one at a time, and then there was a veritable avalanche of women begging for operations, pleading with the physician to come to their apartments after working hours. "If you'll only help me, doctor, I'll pay you a month's wages."

In the beginning Nadezhda Popova was unprepared for the violent emotional reaction of these city women with unwanted children. A young woman about thirty years old came to her one morning with familiar symptoms—missed period, nausea, etc. Nadezhda Popova did a routine examination, and confirmed the obvious diagnosis.

"Well, citizeness," she said, "you are pregnant. I trust you will have a fine baby. Now you come to see me regularly. The nurse will give you instructions on taking care of yourself, and how often to come in."

The woman began to weep. "Doctor, please do something for me. We can't afford another child. We have two already. We can't feed any more. Besides, we have only one room. Where will we put the baby? Please, doctor, give me a pill or do an operation. I will pay you whatever you ask. Please."

Nadezhda Popova's immediate reaction was one of indignation. Imagine someone not wanting a baby. She was trained to bring babies into the world, not to destroy them. . . . But the sight of the weeping woman and her obvious intense distress stilled this indignation. Yet she could not help her. She consoled the woman, saying, "Don't worry, my dear. You will find a way."

(It was obvious the woman didn't believe her.) "Besides, you know that abortions are now illegal. I could get six to ten years. I could not risk such a thing."

She helped the woman to her feet and led her to the door. As the woman passed the other women waiting for consultation, it seemed to Nadezhda Popova that all of the other women interpreted immediately the meaning of the woman's sobs, and that they conveyed to her their sympathy.

Such events became routine. City families had neither the food nor room for children. What should have been a cause for joy became a tragedy in the families of workers, and even among some of the better paid of the white collar class and intelligentsia.

Gradually a new phenomenon appeared—self-administered abortions, followed by infection and sickness. Her first contact with such a case occurred in the middle of a routine day. Nadezhda Popova had just finished an examination of a patient in the seventh month of pregnancy. She entered her notes in the case record while the patient rearranged her clothes and pulled herself heavily to her feet in preparation for leaving.

"Your maternity leave starts next week. Now just take care of yourself, and soon you will have a fine baby."

She walked to the door with the woman, each murmuring polite farewells. Nadezhda turned to the next patient in line, asking her to step into the office.

The patient was a woman in her mid-thirties, an office worker from her dress and manner. She walked slowly and unsteadily to a chair, and began to speak hesitantly. "For maybe two or three months I didn't get sick, so I thought I was going to have a baby. Then last Saturday I had very bad pains in my abdomen. Cramps much worse than my period. Sunday I started to bleed. Then about Tuesday I started to feel very bad; I couldn't go to work. They sent a doctor to see me, and she told me to come in and see you . . . and . . ."

The woman did not continue, whether from sickness or fright it was hard to tell.

"All right, get up on this table and let me have a look at you."

Helping her onto the examining table, Nadezhda Popova noted how hot and dry the woman's skin was. She was running a very high fever. She began the examination and found, as she had expected, evidence of surgical intervention. Obviously this was no spontaneous abortion.

"Let's get down," and she helped the woman back to the chair. "I'm afraid you will have to go to the hospital for a while. You are very sick."

Suddenly the enormity of the situation struck her: this woman might die from the infection. How could she do such a thing? In a burst of anger, she shouted at her, "I don't see how anyone can be stupid enough to do what you did. Don't you know you could have killed yourself?"

The woman broke into tears. "But, doctor, I didn't do anything. I just got cramps and started to bleed."

Her anger subsiding, Nadezhda Popova looked at the sobbing woman. She thought—Oh, what's the use? She'll never admit having done it. If she did, it would only mean trouble for her. Maybe some doctor did it. It would mean a prison term and the loss of her license. . . .

"My God, doctor, please believe me. It happened by itself. If you tell them I did it, I'll be sentenced. Please, doctor, don't do that."

"All right, all right, stop worrying. So it happened by itself." She filled out the necessary instructions. "Take this to the nurse in the corridor, and she will see that you get to the hospital. I'll see you there in the morning."

The woman rose and wavered slowly out through the door. Nadezhda Popova watched her without even rising to help. What a pitiful situation, she thought. Women who want babies, and don't want them. Doctors who should help people, and can't. All this work to become a specialist in helping people to have babies only to be faced with the horror of multitudes of terrified women for whom a child spelled disaster. Women who risked death rather than have babies. . . .

Such experiences corroded her beliefs and principles. Other doctors, she knew, gave in to the pleas of such women and performed illegal abortions out of a mixture of pity and their own desperate need for fees. She resisted stubbornly, refusing to become involved in an illegal act.

But she became more and more wavering in her resistance—until one day she too capitulated. She could never understand what prompted her to say "Yes." It was a simple, relatively unmoving case compared to many others. The wife of a young engineering student who was supporting her husband while he finished his training came in. She said quite casually that she understood Dr. Popova was a very capable obstetrician, and she would like to arrange for an abortion to be performed privately.

Why did she consent, she wondered. What was it? Fatigue from having said "No" so often? Rising resentment at the plight of such people that had reached a point beyond her toleration? The fact that in some way she identified herself with this young girl and could not bear to think of her running the risk of septic poisoning from a self-administered abortion? Perhaps it was an act of protest against the plight of all such women. . . . At any rate, she said: "I believe it can be arranged, but it will have to be done in your own quarters."

The girl hesitated. "My husband and I share a room with another couple. I would have to arrange for them to be away. . . . Perhaps I could meet you at the corner of X. and N. streets at seven o'clock this evening, and if they are not going to be home, we can go to our room."

"Good. We will see each other at seven."

At seven o'clock she approached the corner carrying her black bag with her instruments. The girl was standing there with a stocky, dark-complexioned young man. He shook hands embarrassedly on being introduced. "They will be away," the girl said, "until eleven o'clock. They have gone to the theatre. Please come with us."

They walked briskly for several blocks, and then turned up a street that looked familiar to Nadezhda Ivanovna. She caught her breath. This was the street on which Alyosha lived. Suppose she met him! She looked down at her black bag. What a stupid thing to do. Anyone would recognize her as a doctor on a call! She could have wrapped the necessary instruments and medicine in a towel, and stuffed them in her coat pocket. . . . She hesitated, not knowing whether to go ahead.

The young man noticed that she slowed up. "Are we walking too fast? It's only a few more houses," he said anxiously.

She caught up her step again and rejoined them, only to have her worst fears realized. They were turning into the apartment building in which Alyosha lived! Up the stairs they went, ignoring the elevator which was obviously out of order, past Alyosha's floor, up to the fifth. There they stopped, each panting for breath. The young man fished out a key, opened the door to an apartment, and then unlocked in turn the door to the room which they shared.

What a contrast, Nadezhda thought. Alyosha had an entire three-room apartment to himself. . . .

She asked for hot water. The girl prepared it quickly in the kitchen down the hall. Then she gave instructions, quietly and briefly. The young man stood behind his wife, holding her hands above her head, while she bit her lips to stifle her cries. It was over in a matter of minutes. She told them what to expect, what precautions to take, and instructed them to contact her directly if the girl should start running a fever. That would be better than running the risk of having the case get into the hands of someone who might start an official investigation. They thanked her profusely. The man pulled out an envelope stuffed with rubles, and handed it to her.

She stood looking at the envelope, and was overcome with a burst of shame and guilt. Why *had* she done it? It could not be for money! She could never justify herself if she accepted it. . . . She pushed the envelope back toward him. "No," she said, "I can't take it." She turned sharply and left the room and the apartment.

She started down the hall, searching for the stairs in the dim light. As she picked her way down the stairs she thought fearfully of the possible consequences. And suppose she encountered Alyosha? What would she say? She was on a call, and had gotten the wrong address? She was in the neighborhood and had stopped in to see him, but she had walked past his floor by mistake? . . . Now she was past his floor and on the way out. But there were footsteps coming up the stairs. They were heavy, unsteady, and accompanied by the murmur of a man's voice singing softly to himself. The sounds came from the floor below. It was *his* voice, and then she saw him rounding the stairs, swaying slightly, obviously drunk. Should she speak first? . . .

There was no need. He saw her.

"Well, Nadezhda, healing the sick, I see! Were you looking for me? Come on back and let's have a talk." He took her by the elbow without waiting for a reply and led her back up the stairs and into his apartment.

She was frozen with terror. What would he do? What would he ask? But her concern was misplaced. He was more interested in talking about himself.

"Well, how do you like your old friend Alyosha, huh? Take a look. Even better than it used to be. Look at the new furniture! Look at this suit! Three of 'em I bought this year. Nobody to spend my money on. Why don't you go to concerts with me any more? Too busy healing the sick, I suppose. . . . Well, say something."

"I have been rather busy, Alyosha, and besides I'm not very used to associating with big shots. Why don't you look at *my* clothes once! This is the way a real doctor dresses! With one old coat, a pair of beat-up shoes, two dresses for the winter! That's the difference between being a doctor and a speech-maker. I measure my success by cured patients, not by the number of dresses I buy. . . ." Her fear and shame had all become channeled into rage, and she felt her voice and her anger rise with every stinging word. She broke into an unbridled tirade against Alyosha. He sat growing pale and limp as though both blood and muscle were being beaten out of him. Finally she stopped from exhaustion.

He looked up slowly. She saw for the first time that he was weeping. "I know. I know," he said. "Nadezhda, Nadezhda, not so hard. Have you no pity? We each work in our way." He pointed to her black bag. "You have that; and I have my job too. Don't you know me well enough to realize that I have feelings? But one must learn to master his feelings. It's not easy to make speeches when the words sound hollow to your own ear. If I had it to do over again, I would choose your course. At least you have the satisfaction of helping people. I have to hope that I help in the long run, even though sometimes I have to injure in the short run."

"I'm sorry, Alyosha. You know I am very fond of you, and would not want to hurt you. Perhaps I was too sharp." She walked over to his chair and picked up his hand. She looked down on it, trying to remember in its heavy fleshy mass the hand she had held in their student days. She gazed at the flushed face turned up at her, at the rolls of fat that hung over the collar of his shirt. She caught the heavy fumes of vodka rising from his breath. Somewhere in there was Alyosha. But where? Could she ever find him again? Was he lost to himself?

"You are not pleased with me, Nadezhda!"

"Let's not say that, Alyosha. We have taken different paths, that is all. Good-bye. I wish you good luck."

She turned to go away. He did not speak until she reached the door. "Nadezhda, was it the wife of the student on the fifth floor?"

She looked back and nodded.

"They're nice kids," he said. "I would have done it myself, except I had no confidence. I sent her to you."

Nadezhda stepped quickly through the door, pulling it shut sharply behind her. She ran down the stairs and out into the street. What had happened to them? She an abortionist, and Alyosha a drunkard!

In the years that followed she directed her feelings of fear, guilt, sorrow into her work, and devoted herself even more intensely to the welfare of her patients. She saw Alyosha from time to time, making a speech when a new clinic was opened, or a picture of him in the newspaper addressing a meeting of scientific workers convened to pass a resolution in favor of some new campaign. Occasionally they saw each other closely enough to say hello. As the years progressed, he advanced further, looked more prosperous and more dissipated, and made more pompous speeches. She remembered from time to time his gesture at her black bag, and heard his voice saying: "You have *that*. At least you have the satisfaction of helping people."

It is true, she reflected, I do have that, and as long as I have it, I can still help people in difficulty. . . .

The Party Secretary

Teplov rubbed his eyes to keep awake. It was midnight and he wanted to go home to bed, but years of service in the Party apparatus had taught him the necessity of careful paper work. He was preparing an agenda for the meeting of the Executive Committee of the Raion Party Committee in the morning, and this was no time to make mistakes. It was one of those periods in which any action could have the profoundest political ramifications. Teplov was a technician first, and a politician second, but in a time of crisis politics inevitably saturated all of life.

Stalin's picture still hanging on the wall symbolized the instability of Teplov's world, which would not be peaceful until another picture hung in its place. But whose picture would it be? And when would it happen? It was risky to take sides, and it was risky not to take sides.

Kornetsky, the sardonic Second Secretary, had chanced into the office one day as Teplov was putting a picture of Malenkov in his desk drawer. "We must be prepared for any eventuality, eh, Antip Trofimovitch? One must also be careful that he does not put in the same drawer the picture of two incompatible persons. This might prove to be a very serious business," Kornetsky had commented.

Teplov had looked up, angered. But he did not know how to respond to Kornetsky. He searched the Second Secretary's face

Рисунок А. БАЖЕНОВА.

— Вот, товарищ ревизор, отчёт о нашей работе...
— Хорошо, я учту его содержание.

—And here, Comrade Inspector, is the account of our work. . . .

—Splendid. I will take due note of its contents.

KROKODIL

for some trace of expression that would give him a clue as to what was on his mind. Kornetsky's teeth were fastened firmly on the huge pipe which he seldom smoked, but which was as fixed a feature of his face as his nose and ears. It gave his face a rigid, graven appearance that betrayed no feeling. Teplov muttered and slammed the drawer shut in embarrassment. If things turned out wrong, Kornetsky could use even so small an incident against him.

Many times in the course of the day, he looked at the door of the office and his name in reverse through the glass "A. T. Teplov, First Secretary, Baltinsk Raion Committee." When he did, the same unspoken question came to his mind that came when he looked at Stalin's picture. The sign painters weren't very skillful, but it took very little effort to scrape a name off the door and re-place it with another—no harder than changing Stalin's picture on the wall.

But worrying about such things was a luxury a busy man could not afford. The life of the Raion was dependent on Teplov, and Teplov was dependent on the life of the Raion. If the Raion did not develop, flourish, and produce, he would have failed, and his career would be over. There was little he could do about the fight that was raging among the big shots, but his responsibilities to the Raion were many and immediate. He returned to his task, and was working furiously when he heard a tap at his door.

"Yes?" he called out, wondering who would be calling on him at this hour.

It was Shvartz, the Third Secretary, young, thin-faced, bookish-looking . . . probably, Teplov thought, because of his pince-nez, an incongruous affection for a Party worker. Teplov thought Shvartz looked like Trotsky with a shave. He was a good fellow, though, and a hard worker.

"Well, Antip Trofimovitch," Shvartz said, "I see you're still working."

Teplov gestured silently, drawing his hands across the pile of work on his desk with a single sweeping motion. "How about you?" he asked.

Shvartz grimaced. "I had a class for the four new Party candi-dates. I'm leading them patiently by the hand through the Short

History of the Communist Party. A lazy bunch—I thought they'd go to sleep."

"Well, keep them at it," Teplov answered, and returned to the work on his desk.

Shvartz seemed unperturbed by being cut off so shortly by his chief. He said, "Good night. I'll see you in the morning," closed the door behind him and turned to leave the building. On the way out he noticed a small light bulb burning in one of the offices —and right in the middle of the campaign to save electricity, he groaned as he stepped inside for a moment to turn it off.

"A funny chap, the old man," Shvartz mused as he left the building. "You'd think he'd be more interested in the job I'm doing. Political education is an important part of the Party's work."

Teplov in turn was reciprocating Shvartz's compliment. He smiled slightly as Shvartz closed the door behind him. "A funny chap," he thought, "like one of the enthusiasts from the early thirties or even the twenties."

Teplov was interested in political education, but not in the way that Shvartz was. Teplov wanted the Party and Komsomol members in the Raion to be sufficiently literate in the political classics and sufficiently up-to-date on the Party line so that they would not commit embarrassing errors. And he wanted Shvartz to keep the general populace at a sufficient level of apparent enthusiasm so that there should be no unfavorable reports going into the Center about morale in the Raion.

The Soviet state was built on deeds, not on words, but even a practical man had to have a proper respect for the role of persuasion. It took years of experience and a long process of ripening to appreciate the delicate balance to be maintained between persuasion and coercion. Many young men and women tended to regard persuasion as a façade. The young Party worker who read in the papers the endless telegrams from "workers committees" pledging production goals and contributions often became cynical. He had been assigned the task of securing such "voluntary" actions. He would be told in advance by the Party what action should be taken. Then he would announce at the appropriate point in the meeting, "The adoption of such and such a program recommends itself to this meeting." Everyone understood "it recommends itself" meant "the Party wants." Nevertheless it was possible for the Party, in this manner, to direct affairs while retaining the façade of "democratic" action.

But some young Party workers never realized how this balance of coercion and persuasion worked. On Teplov's desk lay a note which read simply, "New Partorg for shoe factory." If Shvartz tended slightly to overestimate the importance of words, the former Partorg at the shoe factory had underestimated it badly. He was assigned the task of securing a ten percent voluntary contribution to the state loan from the workers of the plant. With guileless naïveté he had posted an announcement that ten percent would be deducted from their pay envelopes . . . without an agitation program in the shop to explain the need of the State for the funds . . . without calling a factory meeting at which the activists among the workers could pledge the required amount. He was so gauche as to assume that everybody knew this was a formality and that it served no purpose. His action caused a furor in the Raion Committee. At Teplov's direction the head of the industrial section called the young man in, gave him a good dressing down, and returned him full-time to his job of running a stitching machine in the factory. Now they would have to select a new Partorg— one with a greater sense of delicacy and of proper form.

Teplov's raw material for preparing tomorrow's agenda was the pile of crumpled slips of paper lying before him. It was difficult to keep in a supply of note pads. But for Teplov this was an item of utmost priority, and he used his connections in Moscow to make certain that two or three times a year a small package of these pads would be sent to him. It seemed like a small item, but without them he was convinced that he would never be able to keep the affairs of the Raion straight. There was no telling when and where some matter of urgency would be called to his attention. He would scribble an elliptical note, understandable only to himself in most instances, tear off the slip of paper, and "file" it in his jacket pocket. In the course of days these slips would migrate from pocket to pocket, and through the various sections of his desk as he took action on these bits of business.

There was one slip in the pile before him which bore the legend, "Chairman, Broad Meadows Kolkhoz." It had started out in his breast pocket, where he kept the note pad, two days before in the morning. He was on his way out of the building when he met the head of the agriculture sector, Nikitin. Nikitin was upset and agitated. He was running his hand around the back of his neck, inside his open collar—a gesture Teplov had long ago identified as meaning that there was trouble, and trouble for which Nikitin was afraid he himself might be held responsible.

"Antip Trofimovitch," Nikitin began, "you'll just have to call the Oblast office again about the chairman at Broad Meadow. They're two weeks behind in sowing, the buildings are in terrible shape, and half the chickens are sick. I can't do a thing with them. Always he gives me nothing but excuses. He should be replaced. We told them that last year."

Teplov nodded slightly, and pulled out his inevitable pad on which he made this brief notation. It was true that they had recommended replacing this chairman. Broad Meadows had been a problem for several years. The chairman was a former brigadier who had gone into service and had a good war record. He joined the Party during the war, and when he returned home the Raion Committee had recommended him for chairman of the kolkhoz. This was before Teplov's time, and he had since suggested tactfully to the Ministry of Agriculture that the chairman should be replaced. Well, this time he would be more firm.

But he couldn't let Nikitin get off that easily. He might get the idea that he could blame everything that went wrong in the agricultural sector on the kolkhoz chairmen. Anyway, he looked like he expected a bawling out. So Teplov gave him a thorough tongue lashing, ". . . passing the buck . . . don't expect me to bail you out of all your problems . . . should have worked more closely with him . . . making excuses is not planting grain." Nikitin grew red-faced, as several people passing by slowed their step to hear the dressing-down he was getting. At first he tried to stem the flow of Teplov's abuse with protestations of *"but, Antip Trofimovitch."* Teplov greeted each "but" with a fresh onslaught. It wasn't until Nikitin gave in and answered repeatedly *"Yes,* Antip Trofimovitch" that Teplov finally let him off.

The slip moved to the top of his desk that afternoon. He placed it there so that he would not forget to call the Ministry. The

Ministry agreed to replace the chairman, and the slip moved to the top drawer of the desk with a number of other personnel problems that he had to take up with the head of the cadres section.

After that he called the head of the cadres section to his office and presented him with a list of positions which had to be filled in organizations under their jurisdiction. He instructed the head of the cadres division to prepare a list of recommendations from the card file, and then shoved the slip, along with the other notations on personnel matters, into his right-hand pocket.

Now, after its long migration it was back out on the desk top where he had emptied his pockets and desk drawers in an effort to restore some order to his records. He made an entry on the agenda, under "Personnel," "Chairman, Broad Meadows." Above it, the list read: "Principal, School #3, Director of Cooperative Store, Z. village, and Partorg, Shoe Factory." Then the slip and its companions were crumpled in one broad gesture and thrown into the waste basket.

He worked his way patiently through the pile of notes. There were a few production problems in several of the small factories in the Raion, but thank God, not many. Nikitin, as head of the agricultural sector, would have to give them a report on the progress of the crops. Also a general propaganda and agitation program would have to be worked out in connection with the recent arrest of Beria. The editor of the Raion newspaper had taken his cue quickly, and of course printed the editorial that had been broadcast from Moscow. But the entire resources of the Raion would have to be mobilized.

Finally, about one-thirty, he finished. It was a warm July evening. Teplov wore a light coat as he walked home. His house was less than a quarter-mile from the office. Baltinsk, after which the Raion took its name, was a small provincial settlement. The streets were unpaved. There was a crude telephone connection with the nearest city. Electricity had been introduced only in the years after the war. As Teplov strolled along under the night sky, he was surveying his capital, for indeed this rural town was the center of the area over which he held sway.

But, now that he was no longer working, his feeling of uneasiness returned. The decision to seek a career in the Party apparatus was a risky one, although it hadn't seemed so to Teplov at the time. He was an engineering student, son of a foreman in a textile plant. His mother was a peasant who had come to the city to work in the same factory in which she met his father. It has seemed quite natural for him to enter the Komsomol, and quite natural for him to accept the assignments which were given him. Before he realized it, shortly after graduation he was no longer an engineer, but an "apparatchik," a member of the Party apparatus. First he was Party Secretary of the plant in which he had shortly before been a junior engineer; then head of the industrial sector in a Raion Committee; an interruption for the war, when he served as a political officer to a regiment and was wounded; and then he returned to be second, and, finally, first secretary of the Baltinsk Raion. Teplov had not been a very distinguished youth. He was a little more energetic than average, a little above average in intelligence, and below average in imagination, but that was more an asset than a liability. He was very little concerned with politics, but quite intent on making a career for himself, and was entirely content to do what was asked of him in order to attain that goal. He was a technician-bureaucrat in a world of politics. As much as possible he tried to stay apart from factional struggles within the Party, and by a considerable adroitness at evading issues he managed to survive a full dozen years in the Party without becoming identified as anybody's man.

But tonight he was worried. It was comforting that he was not involved in any of the contending factions in the Party. He could be sure that he would not automatically be liquidated if the wrong faction won. But, at the same time, he could not be sure of the support of any of the factions either . . . and even though he had no one group of enemies, he did have individual enemies. Particularly he knew that he had enemies in some of the agencies in Moscow, and in some of the central Party offices.

Relations with the Center were always difficult for anyone with a responsible position in the provinces. Not only was the Center forever putting unreasonable demands on you, but they had completely fantastic notions of how to do a job best. Teplov was primarily concerned with his own self-interest and with compiling a record which would in the long run reflect to his credit. But he was strongly identified with his own Raion, and was convinced that neither he nor the country would prosper if the Raion were not in good running order.

Perhaps his worst enemy was V. N. Rashevsky, now a fairly high official in the Kremlin. Rashevsky had been head of the Oblast industrial sector when Teplov was appointed to head the Raion industrial sector. They had a number of arguments—an act of rare audacity on Teplov's part since he was little given to open displays of resistance.

While Teplov was away at war he heard that Rashevsky had been appointed First Secretary for the Oblast. Fortunately for Teplov, Rashevsky moved on to Moscow before he returned. There was little doubt that if Rashevsky had been Oblast Secretary at the time of Teplov's appointment, it would not have gone through.

Teplov rose in the Raion on the basis of his energetic work. But he continued to have his brushes with Rashevsky, who was now in the agricultural sector of the Central Committee.

On one occasion a division of troops was moved into Teplov's Raion. They were authorized to draw on Raion food resources for subsistence. It was quickly clear that the Raion's resources were inadequate. And they had to make the regular grain deliveries in addition! There would have been rebellion on all the kolkhozes, and the workers in the towns would have been short of food. Teplov carried the fight to the Oblast Committee, insisting that the regular deliveries be reduced accordingly, and the new Oblast Secretary took the matter up to Moscow. It was only later, after the matter had been settled in his favor, that Teplov heard that his old antagonist, Rashevsky, had been behind the original order. Incidents like these preyed on his mind.

Still in an uneasy reverie, he arrived at his house, a small, four-room structure, with two bedrooms, a kitchen, and a living room. His wife was sleeping in one bedroom and his two boys in the other. It was typical that he should return home after the family was asleep. He occasionally lamented how little he saw his family. But, except for being deprived of his company, they were well provided for. They were well dressed, housed, and fed. You could tell them by their more prosperous appearance if you saw them in any gathering. His boys, together with the children of the few highly placed officials in the town's two factories, were regarded with deference by their schoolmates. They were growing up with the self-assuredness and cockiness of the kids of well-off parents. Their mother indulged them, and the militia in the town were afraid to discipline them. Teplov paid little attention to them except on infrequent vacations, or when their behavior precipitated some special "scandal" in the town. Then he would lecture them severely. But they sensed that his concern was for the difficulties that their misdemeanors caused him personally, and they became only more skillful in having their way without having their escapades come to their father's attention.

Teplov slipped into bed, and dropped off to sleep. He did this so quickly and quietly that his wife, Elena, was not disturbed. He slept well. In fact he always slept well. He drained so much of his energy into his job that he had no trouble falling asleep even when he was worried.

Teplov knew nothing from the time he hit the bed until his wife shook him awake at eight o'clock in the morning. The children were already eating breakfast. He drew his clothes on mechanically and shuffled to the table. A glass of hot tea and a piece of rye bread sat before him. He gulped on the tea and chewed the bread, and by his own exertions came awake gradually. As he passed from sleep to wakefulness, the voices of the boys advanced out of the background of his consciousness. They were engrossed in the model airplane that Sasha, the older boy, was building. But before Teplov could enter into the conversation, they were busily wiping their mouths on their sleeves, and hurrying off to school.

Elena had already left the table. She cleared a space in the sink, and poured hot water from the tea kettle into a shallow pan that stood beneath a small mirror. Elena placed his razor beside the pan, and went to straighten out the bedroom while he shaved. She came through the kitchen several times while he was shaving, and commented on various household problems, but she seemed to address him only at such disadvantageous moments that he could only grunt through his clenched lips. He slipped into his jacket, said good-bye, and started for the office.

His driver was waiting outside the house sitting in the car and reading the copy of the Raion newspaper which he picked up regularly for Teplov every morning. They exchanged good-mornings, and Teplov got into the back seat. The driver handed Teplov the newspaper.

Teplov was doubly interested in the paper. On one hand he was responsible for it, just as he was responsible for virtually everything that happened in the Raion. Therefore, he was anxious to see that it carried out policy properly. On the other hand, it told him of what was happening in the world outside the Raion. Of special interest were the items which Moscow sent out by radio to be printed verbatim. Occasionally when he had an evening to himself he would sit at home and listen to news stories and editorials being dictated at slow speed over the radio. Particularly in recent months the ponderous voice of the announcer would frequently intone statements reflecting the tremendous changes which were taking place: ". . . comma who has repeatedly committed anti-state activities comma has been taken into custody period" . . . "the doctrine of one-man rule comma which is completely contrary to the principles of the Party comma must be replaced by collegial decisions" . . . "a series of benefits colon lowered food prices semicolon an ever increasing standard of living semicolon . . ." These dispatches were like the acts of some unknown being who would suddenly and violently intervene in Teplov's life, sometimes doing good and sometimes doing evil. *"Deus ex machina,"* Shvartz had commented to Teplov on one occasion when the arm of the secret police had opportunely removed a member of a ministry who was causing them great difficulty. Teplov listened attentively to Shvartz's explanation, and for once was not bored with the Third Secretary's bookish references. He agreed with Shvartz that such events were very much like the timely appearance of the gods in a Greek play—but one never knew in these days on whose side the gods would intervene. He scanned the paper with mixed feelings of anticipation and anxiety, but there was little of interest.

As the car pulled up in front of the Raion headquarters, Teplov noticed an automobile sitting in front of the building. He recognized one of the chauffeurs from the shoe factory waiting in the car. For a brief moment he was puzzled, then he remembered that an inspector from the Chief Administration was expected. The factory had sent the car to the nearest railroad station to meet him. It was covered with dust from the hundred kilometers of dirt road that connected the town of Baltinsk with the railroad.

The inspector, Boris Aleksandrovitch Davidenkov, was waiting in Teplov's office. A round-faced, stocky man, his clothes marked him for a member of the Moscow bureaucracy, but their disheveled condition also showed the effects of his trip. He jumped up smiling, and pumped Teplov's arm warmly. "Just came in to see how the plastic soles are working out on the shoes, Antip Trefimovitch!" he said. "Needn't get scared. No charges of sabotage or anti-state activity." He guffawed loudly at his own joke.

Teplov grimaced and barely succeeded in looking amused. The inspector was a good fellow who caused no difficulty for the Raion, but his macabre jokes provoked little laughter from Teplov. However, his overactive sense of humor was coupled with a general talkativeness, and he brought Teplov many juicy bits of gossip from Moscow. For this Teplov was grateful. The bits of information he picked up from people like Davidenkov who traveled from place to place and brought the news that circulated by word of mouth in the big cities helped Teplov fill in the missing pieces in the pattern which he was constantly trying to put together from newspapers and radio.

"Good morning, Boris Mikhailevitch, I'm delighted to see you," Teplov replied. "I understand things are going fairly well with the plastic soles out at the shoe factory. They had a little trouble with the stitching machines at first, but I think that's pretty well in hand now. . . . But you can see for yourself when you visit the plant. Tell me, how are things in the Ministry?"

"So-so. Too many changes for comfort. But it looks pretty good. Looks like they're going to ease up on the pressure for once. At least you don't hear people going around screaming about raising the production quotas like they were before. Maybe we'll get a little peace."

"What's happening to my old friend Rashevsky?" Teplov asked.

"Oh, is he an old friend of yours?"—Davidenkov had missed the irony in Teplov's tone.—"Well, I guess you're in luck. The rumor is he's going to be head of the cadres division of the Central Committee. It looks like you're in for a promotion. Rashevsky's in with the right people now."

Teplov's head swam. There was no worse place to have an enemy . . . unless it was in the secret police itself, and even they were under attack these days. There was no worse place.

But his face and voice showed little of his feelings. The more you revealed about yourself and your weakness, the more weapons you put into the hands of your enemies. He rose and shook hands with Davidenkov: "I suppose you're in a hurry to get out to the factory. I hope you will drop in here afterward and let me know what you think of how things are going here. I hate to rush you out, but you'll miss the director if you don't hurry. He's due here for a meeting of the executive committee at ten o'clock."

Davidenkov shook hands, and left. Teplov took care of several bits of routine business, but the threat of Rashevsky lay in the back of his mind, and as time for the meeting came closer he found himself ever less able to concentrate on the problems immediately before him. Under ordinary circumstances the worst an enemy in the cadres division could do would be to get one demoted or, in extreme cases, removed from the Party apparatus entirely. But there were always jobs outside the apparatus, and it was rare to have the displeasure of even a powerful person follow one that far unless there was some political charge he could pin on you. But in a time of crisis everything was political. The mere fact that he was not strongly aligned with the dominant faction at the moment could be used to make it appear that he was unreliable; then anything could happen.

Shvartz arrived about five minutes early for the meeting. He was followed quickly by several other members of the executive committee. By the time the clock on the office wall struck ten all the members of the Committee were present except three: Kornetsky, the Second Secretary, Voronsky, director of the shoe factory, and Blonsky, the editor of the Raion newspaper.

Teplov gave an impatient glance at his watch. As he did so, his secretary opened the door and said: "Comrade Blonsky's secretary just called and said Comrade Blonsky will be here in a few minutes." That left just Voronsky and Kornetsky to be accounted for. Voronsky, he supposed, had been delayed by the inspector. "Does anyone know where Kornetsky is?" he asked of no one in particular. No one knew. It gave Teplov a particular feeling of uneasiness that Kornetsky should be absent. There were rumors that Kornetsky was a strong supporter of Rashevsky. He had been transferred to this Raion while Rashevsky was Oblast Secretary, and Teplov knew that there had been suspicious leaks of information. . . .

At five minutes after ten Kornetsky and Voronsky arrived together. Teplov's hand trembled slightly as he shook hands with Kornetsky.

"Sorry to delay things, Antip Trofimovitch," Voronsky said. "But Davidenkov got to my office at twenty to ten, and I couldn't get away sooner. Comrade Kornetsky was with me at the time and we were both held up. That Davidenkov is too damned talkative. We couldn't get away from him. He had to give us all the Moscow gossip before he would let us leave."

Teplov picked up a pencil and quickly began to make a series of notes. He had the impression that Kornetsky was watching him closely, and he was afraid that the tremor in his hand would betray his emotion. Writing kept his hand steady.

Kornetsky's flat voice came from between clenched teeth. "Yes, he told us the news about your old friend, Rashevsky. Big things are happening."

Teplov heard the tip of his pencil snap. For a moment he had no feeling. There could be no doubt but that Kornetsky's use of the phrase "old friend" was deliberate irony. Had Kornetsky heard the pencil break? It sounded to Teplov as loud as a rifle shot. He slipped it into his pocket. He glanced up at Kornetsky, but again the Second Secretary's face was a mask, with the huge pipe sticking out from his mouth. Damn it, muttered Teplov to himself, I wish at least he'd put some tobacco in that goddamned furnace.

"Yes," Teplov answered, "Rashevsky is a very excellent man. He will do a very good job. However, I believe we had better get on with the meeting, since Comrade Blonsky will be delayed for a few minutes."

Teplov turned to the chief of the cadres section. He was not a member of the committee and ordinarily would not be attending the meeting, but since there were so many personnel decisions to be made, he was sitting in. Teplov asked him to present his recommendations. He began with the job of the Partorg in the shoe factory. He suggested a young foreman who had been a member of the Party for about three years. He had a good Party record, was an excellent worker, and seemed to be ambitious to move ahead in the Party.

Kornetsky objected: "He is a valuable worker. The shoe factory is one of the pilot plants developing the use of synthetic soles for the entire country. It cannot spare the services of so valuable a workman."

Teplov was dumbfounded. What was behind Kornetsky's protest? The job of Partorg in the shoe factory was not sufficiently important to take the man off his regular job more than part time. If it were a big factory with hundreds of Party members, Kornetsky's objection might make sense. Then there might be a full-time Party Secretary and he would have to be pulled off production. What, Teplov wondered, can Kornetsky be up to. Ordinarily he would have given Kornetsky a thorough dressing-down for such stupidity. But maybe this time there was more behind his protest than met the eye. Teplov turned his eyes questioningly toward Voronsky, the factory director.

Voronsky was flustered. He stammered and could not answer immediately.

Kornetsky cut in, and continued: "We must be extremely careful with our personnel decisions. At the present time even such an appointment as this may be reviewed by the cadres division of the Central Committee. But, of course, I defer to the judgment of Antip Trofimovitch."

Teplov began to perspire. So this is the game, he said to himself, he's going to make enough of a protest to get himself on the record, let me push the appointment through, and then use this as a lever to get me out by going to Rashevsky with it. Teplov fumbled for words, but before any could come to his lips, there was a noise in the hall, the door flew open, and Blonsky, the editor of the paper, bustled in. Blonsky was a short, round man, who waddled somewhat when he walked. This, coupled with the abnormal energy with which he propelled himself forward, gave him the appearance of an agitated duck. He was flourishing a sheaf of papers. "Sorry, sorry, gentlemen," he said. "Big news from Moscow. I had to wait around to make sure the stenographers got it off the radio correctly. Here it is, Antip Trofimovitch." He tossed the papers down on Teplov's desk.

Teplov glanced at the dispatch. This time there was no mistaking the fact that his hand shook. The men in the room watched him, waiting for some comment.

Teplov read the dispatch aloud:

"A group of enemies of the Soviet state have been arrested for a plot to capture key positions in the Central Committee of the Party itself. These scoundrels, supporters of Lavrenty Beria in his anti-state activities, had wormed their way into influential posts in the Party apparatus. They planned to effect their dominance over the Party by securing positions from which they could influence the appointments of personnel. A major step in this plan was to promote to the position of chief of the cadres section . . ." Teplov paused and stole a glance at Kornetsky. Kornetsky's pipe was not in its accustomed position. He had it in his hand and was stuffing it energetically with tobacco. Teplov continued: ". . . V. N. Rashevsky. Rashevsky, knowing that he could not escape from Soviet socialist justice, took his own life yesterday evening. All other members of this bandit clique are in custody."

Teplov put the dispatch down. "The rest," he said, "just gives some details. Well"—he paused—"I suppose we had better get on."

He turned back to the chief of the cadres section. "I think we can take that man as Partorg. Now, how about the rest of the list?"

The man continued his report, but Teplov found himself not listening to the words. How much politics were beyond one's control! How arbitrary, unpredictable, uncontrollable, unexpected were such events. How powerless one felt when the gods quarreled among themselves. What, he asked himself, was that expression Shvartz used. . . . Oh, yes, *Deus ex machina* . . . like a god coming out of a machine, to lift the threat of politics from him and let him get back to the business of running the Raion.

He glanced again at Kornetsky. Kornetsky was sitting erect, as though listening attentively to the report. Clouds of smoke were billowing from his pipe, and his cheek worked spastically as he puffed furiously on the stem. Teplov reached into the top drawer of the desk, where he found a small knife. He retrieved his pencil from his pocket and began to sharpen it slowly and carefully, letting the shavings accumulate in a small pile in the middle of his desk.

The Housewife

Tatyana Andreyova glanced up from her account book to catch sight of the clock on the office wall. Twenty more minutes until quitting time. She manipulated her abacus rapidly, calculating the total output of toothpaste for the month of April of all the factories under the Ministry's jurisdiction and entered the result in her record. All about her were dozens of other clerks equally busy keeping the statistical records of the Ministry's varied activities. They were mostly women and housewives, and, like Tatyana Andreyova, their minds were only partially occupied with the Ministry's affairs. Mainly they were concerned with planning the evening's shopping and cooking. They were looking forward to the evening with their families and household duties.

Five o'clock finally came and Tatyana Andreyova closed up her work hurriedly, grabbed her coat from the rack in the corner of the office and raced out of the building. She was in a hurry to get to the cooperative store before long queues formed. By the time she arrived, however, several hundred persons were in line in front of each counter. They were more fortunate men and women whose places of work were closer to the store.

Tatyana looked over the lines carefully and got in the queue in front of the meat counter. She was intent on getting a nice piece of veal if possible. Her husband, Foma, had worked overtime a

What Have You Gotten Us Into?

—Comrade architect, you forgot to provide for a door?

—Oh, forget it, forget it. They'll get along.

—It's not the occupants I'm worried about. How will we get
  out?

KROKODIL

good deal in the previous work period and they were feeling prosperous. It would be nice to have a good piece of meat for a
change. As the queue in front of the meat counter advanced
slowly she kept her eyes on the queues in front of the other
counters. She calculated rapidly: fifty or sixty to go before she
got to the meat counter, and the queue in front of the bread
counter was only twenty people long. She addressed herself to
the woman in front and behind her. "Citizeness," she said to
each, "would you keep my place in line? I want to get a few
loaves of bread."

Each of the women gave assent and Tatyana scurried over to
the bread queue. She kept a wary eye on the meat queue, ever
ready to run back if it looked as though her place might reach
the counter before she bought her bread. Things went well. She
got two loaves of black bread, and returned to her place in the
meat queue before it was too late.

But she was disappointed. When she reached the meat counter,
all of the veal and most of the other meat was sold out. Gone to
all those lucky people who have the whole day to shop, she
moaned to herself. She looked over the counter and decided on
a fish of almost a kilo.

From the meat counter she went from queue to queue and
bought a hundred grams of tea, and—God be praised—two bars of
soap. The cooperative store had been out of soap almost a month!
Finally she lined up to get some milk, but she saw the clerk wave
her hands at the line in a final gesture—all gone.

She needed milk for the children. The baby in particular had
to have it. Even though it was already late, she decided she
would try the open market in the hope of buying milk from one
of the kolkhozniks who came in from the country to sell a portion
of the food they produced. As she approached the open market
a score of kolkhozniks crowded around her. They saw the bundles
she was carrying from the cooperative store and thought that she
had brought some goods to trade for their food. When they saw
that she was carrying only her own groceries they lost interest.

She located one ragged old woman with a bucket full of milk.
Tatyana inspected the bucket. It was scandalously dirty and she
decided not to buy the woman's milk. However, after walking

about the market for several minutes she found no one else with milk for sale, and she had no alternative but to return to the woman with the dirty pail. They haggled over the price of the milk, and Tatyana finally ended up paying twice what she would have had to pay in the government cooperative store. The country woman drove a hard bargain, as she knew there was no other milk available at that time of the evening. She poured a bottleful of milk, and Tatyana began on her way home finally, almost two hours after the close of the work day.

Tatyana Andreyova was a relatively tiny woman who moved in a quick and restless fashion, much like an over-animated bird. Her bundles were heavy for her, and the long period of standing and shopping after a full day's work was very tiring. Nevertheless, the prospect of getting home enlivened her and she hurried through the darkened streets to the huge workers' apartment house in which they lived. Foma would almost certainly be playing with the children and waiting for her. Anna, her mother, would probably be in a bad humor over having to wait for supper, but that could be borne. Mother got over her tempers rapidly.

The apartment house in which the Sladovskys lived was a typical example of "modern workers housing." It was built in the early thirties on a relatively modern basis, but it housed perhaps three times as many people as it optimally should. While the design was good, the materials and workmanship were poor. Only a few months after it was opened, two of the steps between the third and fourth floors collapsed and for months the tenants on the fourth and fifth floors had been forced to step across a yawning cavern on the way to their apartments.

As Tatyana Andreyova approached the building three small boys came roaring out of the doorway, with two of them in hot pursuit of the third. She recognized them as the children of families living on the first floor. They were playing their usual game of communist and fascist. The front door was propped open to catch the spring air, and as Tatyana climbed the stairs she noted that the doors to almost all the apartments were also opened for ventilation. Children darted up and down the halls and in and out of the various apartments. Many other wives and husbands, like herself, were coming home late from work, carrying bundles and bottles. One man hurried along the second floor corridor with a squawking chicken grasped by the feet. Still others, who had returned home earlier, were cleaning up the supper debris, and carried baskets and bags of refuse toward the rear of the house.

As Tatyana turned the corner of the second floor landing she caught sight of Sofia Ivanova, a friend whom she had known since childhood. The door to Sofia's one-room apartment was standing open, as were so many others. Tanya saw Sofia clearing away the supper dishes, and Shura, her husband, curled up in the corner with a copy of *Krokodil*. Shura was chuckling, presumably at the cartoon on the back cover. Sofia looked up as Tatyana passed by and waved. Sofia came out and called, "Will you be down in the laundry room later?"

Tatyana answered yes, and the two women agreed to meet there around ten o'clock.

By the time Tatyana had climbed to the fourth floor fatigue began to grip her legs and slow her down. Weariness, cooking odors, a melange of noises ranging from the wailing of an infant to the blaring of radio reproducers, and the frantic movement of playing children and hurrying adults created in her a feeling of deep depression. What a chaotic, disorganized, uncontrollable world, she thought as she stopped for breath at the head of the stairs.

Through the open door of their apartment down the hall, she saw Foma bouncing their sixteen-month-old daughter on his knee. However, Foma looked up and caught sight of her and called to Seryosha who came running down the hall to help her with the bundles.

Tatyana placed her bundles on the table, kissed Foma and the baby and dropped for a moment into a chair. She did not notice immediately that Anna, her mother, was fussing with a pot of tea in the corner.

"Where were you, Mama?" Seryosha asked.

"Where do you suppose she was?" mumbled Anna's voice from the corner. She had mastered the art of mumbling to herself in such a way that one could never tell whether she was speaking to others or merely for her own benefit. She came shuffling forward with a cup of hot tea for Tatyana. "Standing in line, like I told you," Anna continued. "If you want to eat, you have to wait." Then, addressing herself to Tatyana: "I'm sorry, Tanya darling, that you had to do the shopping after work."

Tatyana took the cup of tea gratefully. "Thank you, Mama," she said. "You have to take care of the children. That's help enough."

She took several sips of hot tea, and looked around at her family. The fatigue and depression which had enveloped her at the top of the stairs dissolved, and she felt warm and relaxed in her circle of loved ones.

Tatyana finally replied to Seryosha's question.

"Yes, Seryosha darling," Tatyana said. "Your grandmother is right. I was shopping for dinner. If you will unwrap the fish and get me some potatoes and a head of cabbage from the box on the window sill, I will cook dinner for you."

Suddenly she caught sight of their alarm clock. It read 7:15. Tatyana groaned, "Oh, Lord, Foma! It's the Dryazavins' time to use the stove. I'm late. Seryosha darling," she called after the boy, "don't bother with the potatoes and cabbage now. Will you run down to the kitchen and see if our stove is free or not?"

Seryosha went down the hall to look. Anna looked after him, sadly shaking her head. "See if the stove is free, Seryosha darling. Indeed! See if the stove is free. Before the Bolsheviks we had three big rooms and our own kitchen. We never heard of a communal kitchen. Bah!"

Foma was usually patient with his mother-in-law, but this evening he snapped at her angrily. "Three rooms, you say! Quite right! One for the cattle, one for the chickens, and one for the family."

Anna stopped her muttering and addressed Foma directly. "Don't tell me how we lived. Look what the peasants have today. One room and they have to share that with the cows and pigs. Progress, bah! We lived like kings on our twenty hectares."

Tatyana moved toward the door to close it so that Anna's voice would not carry into the other apartments. Seryosha, however, returned at that moment and sensing that his grandmother was arguing with his father, he closed the door behind him. He looked at his mother and said: "Mrs. Dryazavin is almost through cooking, Mama."

She thanked him, and sought to change the subject of the conversation by asking Foma if he would be home after dinner.

"No, darling," he answered. "I have to go back to the plant for an hour or so. We're having a meeting on norms and quotas for a new operation we're setting up. Old Uzhasnik, the chief accountant, called a meeting. I suspect that all he's really interested in is getting every decision countersigned by two or three other people so that he can pass the buck to somebody else if there's any trouble. He's loaded with ambition, but he's got a brick for a head. Well, where the horse goes prancing, the crab tries to crawl with his claws."

Tatyana accepted this news without too much distress. She had come to take it for granted that Foma would be away from home three or four evenings a week. She was grateful that her own job involved only occasional after-dinner meetings. A rate-setter such as Foma, or any other moderately responsible worker in production, could count on precious little time to spend with his family.

Anna took the baby from Foma, and Foma and Seryosha turned to Seryosha's school work. He was in his second year of school, and regularly brought home arithmetic assignments to do in the evening. Both Foma and Tatyana took great pride in Seryosha's alertness and interest in his studies. They had already planned for him a distinguished career—perhaps as an engineer or a scientist. Tatyana looked fondly at Foma and Seryosha as they bent over the arithmetic book. She took the food and went back to the communal kitchen.

Regardless of inconveniences she knew that her cooking arrangements were relatively good. At least this was better than cooking in the corner of the living room over a primus stove with a single alcohol burner.

Mrs. Dryazavin was taking her cooking off the stove, and preparing to carry dinner back to her apartment. Her small son was there to help her, but as usual he was being a pest to the other women by peering into their pots, sniffing at their food, and asking impertinent questions.

Tatyana noticed that the table and her side of the stove were filthy. Mrs. Dryazavin had left potato peels lying behind her. The table was smeared with the remnants of a rotten onion. And, finally, the soup had boiled over and the stove was a mess. Tatyana's patience snapped, and she grabbed Mrs. Dryazavin from behind as the woman started out the door, almost causing her to spill the food she was carrying.

"You get back here and clean up!" Tatyana shrieked.

But Mrs. Dryazavin was a veteran of such feminine squabbles and Tatyana a novice. Mrs. Dryazavin swore at Tatyana, calling her "a high and mighty bitch," and accused her of "a snot-nosed attitude toward the workers." She told Tatyana that her family was waiting for supper, and she stamped out of the kitchen leaving Tatyana in a speechless fury.

The woman who shared the other two burners of the stove sympathized with Tatyana and helped her clean up the stove and table while her own food was cooking.

"A terrible family," the woman clucked. "You're lucky that you don't have to cook after her all the time. Did you see that fresh kid of hers? Wanted to know if he could have a piece of my meat."

Tatyana was still too furious to carry on a conversation, but the woman continued with her opinions of the Dryazavin clan.

"A terrible family," she repeated. "All of them filthy. The Domuprav told me about them. They're always bothering her for more heat than their share, and they break all the rules of the building. She told me that they kept chickens in the bathtub until the other tenants took them to court . . . terrible people."

Tanya thanked the woman for her help and began preparing her own meal. She cut a head of cabbage into a pot of salted and seasoned water, threw in a meat bone, and prepared a pot of soup. Then she cleaned the fish and set it and half a dozen potatoes to boil in the other pot. With dinner on the stove she quickly cleaned up her own refuse and during the quarter hour it took for dinner to finish, she chatted with the other women in the kitchen.

The woman who had helped her clean up the Dryazavins' mess ordinarily had a different cooking schedule than Tanya, and they knew each other only slightly. They compared notes about each other's family. Tanya learned that her new friend's husband was a lathe operator, and the woman herself was a clerk in a commercial bank. They had three children, two of whom were in the elementary school. The other was not yet old enough for kindergarten and the woman kept the baby in a crèche attached to the bank at which she worked.

Tanya asked her how she liked the crèche.

"It's so-so," the woman answered. "I have to pay about ten percent of my monthly salary. That's not so bad, but the old hag that the bank hires to run the crèche is frightful. I don't like the way she handles the kids, but if I ask questions she gets mad."

"Why don't you put the child in another crèche?" Tanya asked.

"I've thought about it," the woman answered. "But the nearest one is half a mile from the bank, and it's out of my way when I go to work. Besides, Lord knows how long I'd have to wait until I could get the kid in. Well, no matter. My dinner is finished. My man and I are going to the kino after supper. We're seeing a new Czech movie. It's a musical comedy, but I forget the name. A woman I work with saw it and said it was very beautiful."

"Good luck," Tatyana said enviously.

"I'll see you soon," the woman replied.

Tanya's dinner was finished too. She picked up her two pots, tucked the bag with the rest of her potatoes under her arm, and hurried back to the apartment.

Foma and Seryosha had the table set, and a loaf of black bread out. Tanya asked Seryosha not to drink too much milk because they needed it for the baby.

The family sat down and ate hungrily. The fare was simple, but the quantities were adequate. Tanya and Foma were too tired to do other than eat in silence. Seryosha, however, rattled on about school as he ate.

"Mama, we wore our red ties today. We had a big Pioneer meeting with marching, and banners and everything. A very important Komsomol leader talked to us. He said if we learn to march real well we can march in the May Day parade. Won't that be great, Mama? Won't it, huh?"

Tanya smiled at Seryosha's eagerness. Anna commenced mumbling again, and Tanya feared another explosion. "What did you learn in class, darling?" she asked.

"Well," said Seryosha between gulps of soup, "we had arithmetic and history. I learned about adding. And in history we learned about how all the people were slaves before the Revolution. The priests invented a God to fool the working people . . . and that we must thank Stalin for all that we have today."

Anna glared at the boy. "And," she asked, "did the teacher tell you to thank Stalin for holes in your shoes? Such garbage they pour into your ears."

Seryosha looked puzzled, and turned to Foma. "What does Granny mean, Papa? Isn't it true that the Russian people were poor before the Revolution?"

"Yes, of course, Seryosha. Granny just wants to say that there are some poor people today, also. Now finish your soup. We have to clear away the dishes soon."

Supper finished with no further incidents. Seryosha and Anna cleared the table, while Tanya helped Foma on with his coat. It was already eight o'clock and he was due at the plant in half an hour.

As Tanya helped Foma she noticed a new tear under the left arm of his coat. She sized it up with the expertness of one accustomed to patching and mending. It would need a patch, since the cloth around the tear was weak. Foma noticed her concern with the hole, and patted her on the head.

"Don't give it another thought, Tanya darling. I'll be right in style. They're featuring the patched motif this season."

Tatyana gave him a hug. It was such a relief to be married to a man as good-natured as Foma.

As soon as Foma left, Tatyana sent Seryosha off to bed. She and Anna gathered up the dishes and headed back for the kitchen. As they left the apartment they carefully turned off the single forty-watt light bulb with which the room was illuminated. After all, electricity was rationed and the meter carefully fixed to shut off the current if they exceeded their monthly quota. Some of their friends used twenty-five-watt bulbs so that they might cook occasionally on a hot plate. They were alone in the kitchen, and as they washed the dishes Anna began complaining about the way in which Tatyana and Foma were raising Seryosha.

"Praise Stalin, humph," she said in an undertone, keeping her voice low in the manner of a person who is habitually thinking and saying what should not be overheard. "Humph. He should learn a little religion. The Lord knows I do my best. March in a May Day parade, indeed. Does he know about an Easter Parade? If he were my son I would forbid him to join those godless Pioneers."

"Mother," said Tatyana softly. "Do be reasonable. You know how much it means to the boy to belong to the Pioneers, and we do let you teach him a little about religion."

"Precious little. I teach him to pray to God to bless the family. Do you know what he said the other night . . . bless Stalin, too . . . that's what he said."

Tatyana kept her voice down, but turned vehemently on her mother. "Now listen, Mother. You know we feel as you do. But use some sense. Let the kid alone. When he's older he'll find out about things for himself. Do you want us all hauled into court? The first thing you know he's going to blurt out one of your remarks about Stalin, and then they'll want to know where he heard it. Now you learn to hold your tongue or you'll have to go live by yourself. The boy has to live. There's no point in making him unhappy just because we have different ideas."

Tatyana suddenly felt a burst of shame. Instead of fighting back Anna was standing silently, her lips quivering. Tatyana embraced her and wept: "Mamushka, I'm sorry to be angry with you. Please, you know how much we love you. I am so sorry to have been cross with you. Perhaps I am just too tired."

Anna stroked Tatyana's face and said: "It is nothing, Tanya dear. I know you are tired, and besides it may be that I should be more careful around the children. I don't wish to cause trouble."

She picked up a handful of dishes and walked out of the kitchen.

Tatyana followed her mother back to the apartment carrying the remaining dishes. When they returned the baby was awake and crying in the other room. Anna brought the baby a piece of bread to soothe it. Soon the baby's voice died down, and Tatyana heard Anna preparing to go to bed. Tanya reflected how lucky they were to have two rooms. At least she and Foma could have a little privacy, and they could get away from the family once in a while. In this at least they were more fortunate than the majority of their friends, most of whom were crowded into a single room.

She glanced at the clock. It was only nine o'clock. She still had another hour before going down to the laundry room. She spent the time in straightening and cleaning the room, and in mending some of the clothes she was going to wash.

At five of ten Tatyana was finished with her chores about the apartment, and went with her dirty clothing down to the laundry room.

Sofia was already there. She had her clothing in one tub, and was persuading a woman who had just arrived to leave the tub next to her free for Tatyana. The woman agreed pleasantly and took the third tub, which stood somewhat by itself in the corner.

"Any hot water?" Tatyana asked Sofia.

Sofia shook her head negatively. "No. Too late. I asked the Domuprav if she couldn't spare a little heat for us, but she swears we're over our heating norm and she can't give us hot water after nine." Sofia shrugged her shoulders. "There's no point in complaining. We're lucky the central heating is even working. I visited my sister last week and their central heating hasn't worked since before the war. They have a potbellied stove with a pipe sticking out through the window, and now the housing authorities have declared their stove to be a fire hazard. Fine thing. And they have to stack their wood in the room because it gets stolen from their bin in the cellar. . . . Here, Tanya, let me help you put your clothes in the tub."

The two women left the clothes to soak for a few minutes. Sofia produced a battered pack of cigarettes from which she offered Tanya one. Cigarettes were Sofia's luxury, and she insisted on buying fairly expensive ones. She maintained that no woman could possibly endure the tobacco in the low-priced cigarettes that Shura, her husband, smoked.

"Well," Tatyana asked her, "how are things with you and Shura?"

"Fine, Tanya, fine," Sofia answered. "Shura takes his examinations next week. Then we will have an engineer in the family."

"Oh, that's wonderful, Sofia!" Tatyana answered.

Tatyana and Foma had married when Tanya was twenty-two, and they had Seryosha only two years later. Sofia had married about the same time, but had divorced her first husband. He was a handsome young boy from the village, but he was a poor worker in the factory, and had a bad disposition and drank a lot. Then Sofia met Shura, who was beginning to study engineering in the Tekhnikum, and they were married.

Tatyana and Sofia had been friends since childhood and talked to each other with entire frankness. They shared the secrets of each other's marriage, and Tatyana felt almost a sense of personal triumph in Shura's impending graduation. She knew how difficult it had been. Shura worked evenings as a watchman for a long time. Sofia remained lonesomely at home. There were the crises: the year previously they were afraid that Shura would not get his stipend. He had been working so much in the evenings that he had fallen behind in his studies. Then there was the time two years ago when Sofia discovered she was pregnant. She called Tatyana into her apartment and wept bitterly. Another mouth to feed would make the difference between Shura's staying in the Tekhnikum or leaving to go to work. Fortunately, Sofia was able to obtain an abortion.

"So, Sofia! We will have an engineer in the family! I suppose you will be leaving us soon."

Sofia grimaced. "Maybe. I don't know. Shura's going to try to get assigned to a plant in the city. He hopes to use me as an excuse. But anyway, this is what we have been working for—his degree. If he gets sent to work in the provinces, well . . . that's that." Then, smiling, she continued. "And maybe now we can afford to have some babies. Shura loves your Seryosha. He would like to have a boy like him."

The woman who had been using the corner tub stepped out for a moment.

Sofia whispered to Tanya almost in a conspiratorial tone. "Tanya, does Seryosha still need shoes?"

"Oh, my, yes. His shoes are in terrible condition, but I can't afford to pay open market prices."

"Our store got a shipment in today, and they go on sale at eight tomorrow morning."

"Oh, no! Sofia, what will I do? I have to be at work at eight. I don't mind queuing up early, but what will I do? I *have* to get to work. I was late once last month. I can't go to jail for a pair of shoes no matter how badly Seryosha needs them."

"Why don't you queue up early and have your mother take your place at seven-thirty? I'd try to get you a pair through the manager, but we have a new one and I don't know him well enough to ask."

"I suppose that's what I'll have to do," Tanya said. "I'll get there at six, and then have Mother come down at seven-thirty . . . I hate to do that to her, especially after the spat I had with her tonight."

"What about?"

"Oh, the usual thing. She was angry about how we're bringing up Seryosha. Maybe she's right, but the boy is young and he has to live his life. . . . Sofia, I hate to fight with her. I love her and we need her. If we didn't have her to take care of the kids and the house I wouldn't be able to work. But I guess we all get tired at times. Even Foma was cross with her tonight."

Sofia nodded sympathetically. "Foma is really an angel, Tanya. And so is your mother. We all have our bad moments sometimes. . . . Well, my clothes are washed. I'd better take them upstairs and hang them up. Shura is waiting for me. Good luck with the shoes!"

"Thanks for telling me about the shipment, Sofia."

Tanya finished the remainder of her washing, and hurried upstairs as quickly as she could. The hour was late, however, and the weight of the clothes and the long day of work burdened her down. She went ever more slowly until finally she reached her floor and tottered into the apartment where she dropped the clothes on the table.

Anna heard her enter and came sleepy-eyed into the front room. Tanya sat sprawled out in a chair. Anna hung the clothes on a line strung across the corner of the room while Tanya sat and explained her plan for getting new shoes for Seryosha. Anna nodded as she hung the clothes and answered that she would be at Store 138 at seven-thirty to take over the place in the queue.

When she finished hanging the clothes, Anna looked at Tanya and suggested that she go to bed. Tanya answered that she would wait up until Foma came home.

Anna looked silently at Tanya. She took the pan of tea which was left from supper, put in a pinch of soda to revive its flavor and went down the hall to heat it. She returned in a few minutes, placed the pan on the table with a cover over it, and set out a large chunk of bread and a glass of jelly. She patted Tanya on the head and went back to bed.

Tanya dozed off and was wakened by Foma returning home at midnight.

"How was your meeting, Foma darling?" she asked.

"Nothing special. Just like I thought. The old boy wants to get everybody's signature onto everything, and put a protest in the record for every idea we have. To hell with him. Let's enjoy our tea."

He poured Tatyana a cup of tea and handed her a slice of jellied bread.

Bubbling with enthusiasm she told him her plans for getting a new pair of shoes for Seryosha. He smiled and, typically, refused to get excited. "Let's hope it works, my darling," he said.

They sat for almost a quarter of an hour enjoying their tea and bread, and each other's company. This was the moment of the day for which they lived, and no matter how tired they were it was worthwhile losing a little additional sleep in order to have a few moments by themselves.

Finally they finished their tea and undressed for bed. Tatyana set the alarm for five o'clock. This meant that she could get to the store by six, which should be early enough.

She slid into bed after Foma. He placed his arm beneath her head, and she kissed him softly on the cheek.

"Foma darling," she whispered, "when I was a foolish, romantic girl I used to dream of building a career with my husband. We would both be rich and famous. I don't worry about the future any more. We have enough to do each day. But I have you and I have the children." She kissed Foma again but he was asleep. It was a shame they were both so tired at the end of the day. . . .

The Fully Equipped Author.

—What are you doing?

—Observing life.

KROKODIL

The Writer

An artist, Comrade Letnik, can never be harnessed to a
collective. He is not a beast of burden to do other men's tasks.
He cannot produce by quota or by norm. What is essential to
the artist is that he must do something that is his own. That
which makes him an artist is the fact that *he must create*. It matters not if it is writing, painting, acting, playing, or composing
music. . . . What is of the essence is that what he creates must
come from within—and it must be his own. It cannot be ordered.
There is something in the artist that compels him to put his own
stamp on the world. Without this he is no artist—merely a technician. . . ."

Rodion Trofimovich drank in every word. He gazed entranced
at his companion. He had never met so violent and eloquent a
young man. If he was typical of the Moscow literary world, it
would indeed be an exciting place.

"Boris Mikhailovich Krotki, poet and assistant theatrical pro-
ducer," the young man had introduced himself when he encountered Rodion Trofimovich tugging his handbags through the
door of his newly rented room. "I am your next-door neigh-
bor." And without invitation he had followed Rodion into the
room and asked him why he had come to Moscow. Rodion explained that he had come to study in the literature faculty of
the university, that he had come from Leningrad, and that he

intended to become a writer. And so his visitor had set out to explain the artist.

As Rodion unpacked, Krotki regaled him with stories of Moscow literary life, of the theatre, of the famous artists whom he knew. He grew more eloquent and aroused as he continued to talk. When he came to the topic of his favorite *bête noire,* RAPP —the Russian Association of Proletarian Writers—he reached such a peak of excitement and activity that Rodion and his bags were crowded out of the center of the room into a corner, and Rodion stopped his attempts to unpack in order to devote full attention to his newly found friend.

"If RAPP has its way, we'll all be caged. The wings of our imagination will be clipped. All of art will be politicized. What do you think will happen if their political dogmatism is enforced?" Krotki paused dramatically, as though waiting for an answer.

"But, Comrade Krotki," Rodion ventured, "aren't you a bit pessimistic? Very splendid things are being done in your own field of the theatre."

"Indeed they are, Comrade Letnik," Krotki answered. "But do not be mistaken as to their source. Remember, it is only a scant ten years since the Revolution, and already the stifling hand of political dogmatism is making its mark. I will speak only of those who are successful—Stanislavsky, Maierhold, Tairov. Why are they so creative? I will tell you! Being deprived of the right to say what they want to say, they experiment with new ways of saying what is permitted. I have worked with them, and I know. We all are turning away from the substance of what we say. We are only trying to create new forms. In the theatre we experiment with lighting, staging, acting. But soon even this will be denied us. By the end of the First Five Year Plan we shall be collectivized too."

In himself and his words Krotki encapsulated the past and the future of Russian art. With his enthusiasm, commitment, and artistic integrity, he epitomized the temporary efflorescence of art during the twenties. But with uncanny accuracy he foresaw what was to happen to art under the Bolsheviks. . . .

Under the guidance of Krotki, Rodion was treated to a brief acquaintanceship with the waning artistic world of the NEP. Krotki introduced him to the devoted writers, painters, sculptors, and musicians who spent their evenings in cafés and each other's rooms fighting and arguing over fundamental questions of art, over their own place in the world of creative expression, and over the relative merits of Russian and Western artists. Maiakovsky shouted out his verse. Rodion took part in open debates about the role of the artist in socialist society. . . .

Then suddenly it all came to an end.

RAPP was victorious. Even though it was officially dissolved, its place was taken by the newly formed Union of Soviet Writers, and the Union enforced the sterile politicizing doctrine that Krotki had feared. Before the First Five Year Plan came to an end Krotki's pessimism was more than justified. Babel, whom Gorki had praised as the writer of the future, was silenced. Olesha's *Envy*, which had been likened to the work of Dostoevski, was condemned by the critics. Maiakovski followed Essenin's cue; he renounced a world in which the artist was forbidden to speak in his own voice and stilled that voice with his own hand.

Krotki, excellent prophet that he was, still insisted on producing a political satire months after official judgment had condemned such plays. He was hailed before the Writers' Union, warned by the secret police, and railed against in the press. In disgust he quit the theatre and took a job as a machinist in a factory.

When Rodion finished his course at the University in 1932, in recognition of his excellent scholarship he was offered a position working with the distinguished folklorist, Professor Smolensky, on a folklore collection of the peoples of the Caucasus. Seeing this as an opportunity to support himself while he became established as a writer, he accepted the post.

In the meantime, he and Boris Mikhailovich Krotki continued to work nights on their own writings, reading to each other as they finished each part. They realized that they were writing things which they well knew could never be published, things which might well bring about their arrest. They cultivated an illicit literary group, whose interests centered around their own unpublishable works and those of such proscribed writers as Essenin, Babel, and Pilnyak.

One evening, Rodion rapped on Krotki's door in great excitement. He had uncovered a treasure in a second-hand store—a volume of Valéry. The dealer, unable to read French, did not realize that the work was outlawed. Krotki snatched the volume from Rodion's hand, opened it almost at random, and began reading from it in subdued tones but with the dramatic delivery of a man of the theatre.

Rodion felt tears well in his eyes as he listened. As Krotki paused in his reading to leaf through the volume in search of other passages, Rodion said impassionedly: "Boris Mikhailovich, we Russians could create like this, and perhaps even better. We could add the Russian feeling for the immediacy of life and our sense of spiritual reality to the formal perfection of the French. We were on the path to that once. But look at us now! We write like schoolboys, by formula and stereotype. Who are our successful writers today? Tedious, pedestrian hacks, unable or unwilling to produce anything more than flat, dead trash. The worker exceeds his norm. The Party Secretary dispenses wisdom. Peasants flock to the collective. All evil stems from kulaks and capitalists. 'Socialist realism,' they call it! What a mockery to use the word 'realism.' To write in the spirit of 'socialist realism' is to lie. It is to lie about the life that was, the life that is—about our Russian world, and about the foreign world. We can never create again if we are to be bound by a formula of lies."

But despite their despair and pessimism they continued to write —and even attempted to publish their work. Rodion hoped against hope that by some freak, perhaps by the inherent quality of his work, he could overcome the bans and limitations on what could be published. He submitted a poem to *Oktyabr,* a poem that had been enthusiastically received by his friends. It was an expression of the loneliness and despair of a man in a large city—

> "I woke to early morning bleakness
> And after-rain puddles of my despair . . ."

The poem was returned with a long letter from the editor explaining that despair and loneliness were not proper feelings for a Soviet citizen.

The editor enclosed a recent copy of the magazine with two poems checked off as suggested examples of "socialist realism" for Rodion's guidance. One was a panegyric: "O Great Stalin." It began:

> O Great Stalin, giver of light,
> O Great Stalin, giver of inspiration . . .

The other was addressed by a Soviet girl to her lover on the collective farm, and entitled "Not Till Victory is Ours." She announced heroically that love could not be theirs until he had exceeded his sowing norms and assured the country of a record-breaking harvest.

After a rebuff such as this Rodion would fall into alternate moods, trying one day to grasp the formula that would make his writings acceptable and bring him the high fees that were given to successful authors; the next day renouncing bitterly any suggestion of compromise and working away feverishly at a short story or poem that he could enjoy by himself or share with his intimates.

It was apparent to everyone that the bloom was missing from the literature of "socialist realism." Even the Party press complained and called for "greater creativity," for "a higher level of artistic quality," for "well-rounded, living characters." Like many others, Rodion took ill-founded hope from statements such as these and attempted once more to produce a novel of artistic merit.

The story was of two brothers, one of whom became a Party member through personal ambition but was a very effective and productive member of the community; the other became a Party member for idealistic reasons but effected only destructive results. The theme he wished to illustrate was that good intentions do not always produce good results, and good deeds may sometimes result from motives which are, at best, ethically neutral. The manuscript came back in a few weeks. The publisher had not even dared send it up to Glavlit for censorship. It was accompanied by a scorching letter of denunciation: "Rotten bourgeois morality . . . decadent ethical principles . . . utterly alien to the spirit of socialism. . . ." A week later Rodion was invited to the headquarters of the NKVD, where he was questioned thoroughly on his social background, his past associations, and very sternly warned that any future attempts to publish such counter-revolutionary literature would be dealt with severely.

Obviously, Rodion said to himself as he left the NKVD building, I have not learned the formula. I do not know what its limits are. If I am to publish, I must forget experimentation. I must learn the formula exactly and write according to it. . . .

And so for some years he had no income from his writings, living entirely on his earnings as a researcher at the University.

Finally the collection of Caucasus folklore was completed, and Professor Smolensky submitted a draft to the Folklore Section of the Writers' Union. Three weeks later Professor Smolensky was notified that there would be a general meeting of all persons connected with the collection of this material. He seemed to be considerably disturbed by the summons, but Rodion Trofimovich was so pleased with the scholarly work done on the volume that he refused to believe that anything could be found wrong with the work. He counted on the continuation of the research work in the University's Folklore Section to support him until his writing succeeded.

The meeting was attended by the chief folklorists, and—to everyone's surprise—by the Secretary General of the Writers' Union, Alexei Stepanovich Krichit. No sooner had the meeting opened than Krichit rose to attack the volume and those persons responsible for its preparation. The folk sayings were left in crude form, without being reworked to exemplify socialist ideals, he said. And many of the sayings dealt with superstitions and religious subjects which were entirely inadmissible in a "scientific" volume. But the greatest fault of all was the almost complete absence of any folk sayings relating to Stalin. . . .

Rodion Trofimovich was petrified. Such an attack could mean anything from loss of a job to being sentenced as a counter-revolutionary.

Professor Smolensky rose. His hands were clenched, his lips compressed so that they seemed drained of blood. "Comrade Secretary, we cannot manufacture folk sayings to order," he said with dignity. "If the people have not invented them, there is little for us to do!"

"Don't give me that rot!" Krichit stormed. "Are you trying to imply that the folk of the Caucasus don't love our Great Leader sufficiently to make him the subject of their folklore?"

Professor Smolensky stood silent for a moment and then said: "I cannot continue as director of the project under these conditions. I resign."

"You resign! What the hell do you mean, you resign?" Krichit was shaking with rage. "You'll resign when I damned well tell you to. You'll have a revision of this stinking volume in my hands in three months or I'll know the reason why. That's all. The meeting is dismissed."

The members of the Folklore Section blanched to hear their most distinguished colleague attacked in this fashion. They filed silently out of the room.

The volume was revised in the scheduled three months, but Rodion Trofimovich never learned how it was done. He resigned his post at the University and left the project immediately after the meeting.

Rodion knew that the fate of his recent novel and his association with Professor Smolensky would make it difficult for him to get a good position in Moscow until time had dulled memories of these events. Many of his friends had left Moscow. Krotki had tried to return to the theatre, but producers were afraid to hire him. Leaving the city, he went on a barnstorming tour, doing readings of plays and poetry in the villages and towns and at rest homes. There was little left to hold Rodion to Moscow. A friend in the theatre section of the Writer's Union had long urged him to take a post as director of one of the small dramatic groups that toured the Ukrainian provinces, and now he decided that this would be a propitious time to accept the offer.

The group was small, comprising only thirty people in all, including twelve technicians. They drew on local citizens for such additional help as they needed—electricians, carpenters, and others. Their repertoire was set by the Oblast Committee in Kiev and included, for the most part, recent plays dealing with kolkhoz life. The Oblast Committee permitted only two classical plays in a repertoire of twenty. The players would usually set up at a large kolkhoz for a period of two weeks and run through the repertoire. The people from the neighboring kolkhozes were brought in trucks to see the performances.

Rodion found that the people resented the new literature as much as the artists did. One day after the performance of a particularly boring play about kolkhoz life an old peasant woman engaged him in conversation as he was leaving the theatre.

"Why is it, batushka," she asked, "that you people always show us the same kind of thing? We work all day in the fields from sunrise to sunset. All we see is cabbages, cows, brigadiers, and other kolkhozniks. Then in the evening, whether it's a movie or a play, we have to look at the same thing. We come to sit and relax—and we see more kolkhozniks, more brigadiers, and we are told to work harder and grow more cabbages. Is that the way to relax, batushka? It only tells me that tomorrow morning I have to work again. Why can't you show us a play of faraway places or past ages?"

Rodion smiled and said that he had his orders.

The old woman shook her head. She muttered as she walked from him: "Ah, if they could get inside my head they'd have me dream all night only of higher norms and more cabbages!"

It was an open secret that the people virtually had to be forced to patronize the new literature and drama, that if left to themselves they returned to the Russian classics and Western literature. In the cities the producers complained that they had to present the classical plays in order to keep their theatres financially solvent. To meet this condition the Party organizations of factories began buying tickets and distributing them free. The workers were even given free bus rides from the factory to the theatre.

Discouraged with the dull routine of the provincial theatre, and hungry for the literary life of Moscow, Rodion decided once more to try writing, hoping to earn enough money to permit him to return to the city. Furthermore, he had fallen in love with Irena Ivanovna, the traveling company's ingénue. She had never been to Moscow, and they talked enthusiastically about settling in that city after their marriage. He found that continual exposure to the monotonous formula had made it part of his very way of thinking. He could depict a kulak as black and villainous as those on the stage of the provincial theatre—or a Party organizer as white and virtuous, a kolkhoz maiden as enthusiastic and energetic, and a tractor driver as imbued with the spirit of mechanization.

Two of his plays were immediately accepted and put into limited production.

Rodion began to lay plans. He and Irena Ivanovna would get married immediately. They decided that he should ask for a three months' leave at an Artists' Rest Home. They would have their honeymoon there while he worked on another play. With three plays in production, and a loan from the Writers' Union, he could return to Moscow and begin a serious literary career. . . .

Permission came for his leave. Rodion and Irena were married, said good-bye to their friends, and set off by rail for the Crimea. Their journey southward began very pleasantly, but was rudely disturbed by news of the Nazi invasion. Not knowing what else to do, they continued on to the Crimea. On their arrival Rodion found that his leave had been cancelled. He had been assigned to organize a group of players to entertain troops at the front.

He and Irena returned to the station to start the trip back north. In Kharkov they assembled their group and headed westward, rehearsing in the railroad car as they traveled toward the front. They were given several new plays on patriotic themes to add to their repertoire. These plays, although hastily slapped together and poor in quality, at least were something different from the usual rubbish.

For four years he and Irena traveled with the troops, retreating and advancing with them, often giving performances within sight of the enemy. For the first time in years he was at peace with his own soul. Most of the plays were bad, but at least they said something that a man could decently hold to—the defense of one's fatherland against the invader.

The impulse to write out of the sheer necessity to express what was in him came to life again. Seated in cold trucks, bouncing over ruts and holes, Rodion wrote with stiffened fingers, bracing himself against Irena on one side and the truck on the other.

He wrote four plays into which he poured the heroism he saw about him. Some things he had to suppress—the penal battalions forced at gunpoint to clear away minefields, the masses of soldiers who deserted in the early period, the pillaging and raping of the conquered population as the Red Army moved into the West. But one could forget such details with good conscience when the main issue was so clear.

His war plays did not achieve the staggering success of some of the big hits, but they netted him many tens of thousands of rubles. Under the pressure of the political organizers at the front most of his royalties went immediately into state loans; but when he returned from the front after the war he found himself with a small savings account and a perceptible reputation in the Writers' Union.

He returned to Moscow and immediately began looking up old friends. Professor Smolensky had never recovered entirely from his difficulties with the Party over the folklore volume. Rodion found him teaching literature in a minor pedagogical institute—a bitter old man looking aged beyond his years.

"Hah," he snorted at Rodion, "do you know what I'm doing now? Teaching the little dears the elementary facts of Russian literature! But I have my own work. I am editing the works of our sixteenth century poets. I trust that they have no political relevance. Nobody can complain about what they wrote about our great leader Stalin. Yes, Rodion Trofimovich," he sighed, "I've joined the internal emigration and I wouldn't enter into the mainstream of Soviet art again even if it were possible. Perhaps for you younger people it is worthwhile. But not for me."

Rodion found that his wartime plays had given him sufficient standing so that he was given entree into the upper strata of the Soviet art world. He met such luminaries as Simonov, Sholokhov, Panova, and the more successful musicians, Shostakovich, Prokoviev, and famous theatrical and movie producers. He entered a new world of people dressed in western-made clothes—of people with large apartments and automobiles, people who had their own summer homes, in some instances two or three. And as he thought about the startling difference between their lives and his own he was spurred on to achieve success.

He threw himself into his new work, a novel of returning veterans. Day after day he rose with the sun and wrote until evening

—writing, rewriting, tearing, discarding, retrieving, and finally reading out loud at the end of the day to Irena or a friend.

The returning veteran in the process of reabsorption into Soviet life furnished Rodion a pretext for introducing multidimensional characters in whom he could be genuinely interested. His hero had an affair with another man's wife, questioned the wisdom of Party decisions and longed for the comforts of German life. Eventually he saw the error of his ways, became an enthusiastic Party member, and settled down to life as a factory foreman. Even though the end of the novel conformed to the requirements of political acceptability, the body of the plot gave Rodion an opportunity for the richness of character development that was so sadly missing from the work of all but a very few writers, such as Vera Panova. It was with considerable excitement that he sent the manuscript off to the publishers.

The publisher's word came in a matter of a few weeks. The novel would be published if he made certain changes—surprisingly few and unimportant, he thought. Next the censors' approval was received from Glavlit, and the story began appearing in installments in the *Literary Gazette.*

The resulting critical acclaim was more than Rodion had hoped for. Several critics praised it as an exemplification of what had been so long demanded of Soviet writers—fully-drawn characters, a plot with imagination, and a sense of reality—all this within the framework of proper socialist consciousness. Arrangements were made for translation and for dramatization. Unquestionably his book was going to be a big hit. Rodion and Irena sat planning what they would do with the royalties.

Then the storm broke. A high Party official wrote an angry letter to *Culture and Life,* pointing out defects in Rodion's novel. "It is incompatible with socialist morality and an insult to our brave soldiers to depict them as debauching their comrades' wives," he wrote. "The Soviet youth are proud of our ever-increasing standard of living, which they recognize as being a product of the socialist order. In this they are in marked contrast to author Letnik with his vulgar fawning before the West. . . . The author's very real talents, as exhibited in his wartime patriotic plays, must not be squandered on such worthless trash as this. Those critics who have praised this work must relearn the lesson of Party vigilance. The publishers are equally to blame and must cease immediately printing this and similar trash which their laxity has permitted to appear in print these last few years. As for Comrade Letnik, he must mend his ways and turn his energies to more worthwhile tasks."

The Writers' Union called a meeting of the main writers and Party personnel whose voices were most important in artistic circles. Rodion Trofimovich sat through four hours of speeches in which his novel was held up as an illustration of all that was wrong in Soviet literature. Finally he had to rise and excoriate himself for more than half an hour. He blamed not only himself for failing to see his errors, but also those critics who had supported his writings. He promised to begin immediate work on "something more suitable."

As he walked away alone from the meeting hall the confusion he had felt since the beginning of the attacks on him came to a climax. What had happened? What could he do? What should he do? How could all this be? The novel was accepted, the critics approved it—and then *this*. Had there been a change in line? Or had the publishers and critics gotten lax? How could you know what to do? Did you have to prostitute your art completely? Even if you did, was there any assurance that something wouldn't go wrong? Evidently even the critics did not know the formula perfectly.

He told Irena what had happened, and assured her that no serious consequences would follow. It was obvious that the Party regarded him as a valuable asset to the regime if he would conform to its demands. But how to conform—that was the question! How to conform. . . . What to do. . . . What to write. . . .

That night he had a dream. He was an eagle, aching to soar into the sky, to soar in exaltation as he felt the full surge of his power. From the height he would perceive the beauty of the universe. He would revel in the freedom of flight. And finally he would achieve his goal—the full realization of his powers, the understanding of beauty. . . . He rose from the ground with his wings extended. Suddenly he was jerked up short and brought crashing to the earth. He tried again and again to fly, but time after time he crashed to the ground as some restraining force pulled him earthward. . . . Finally he heard a voice saying: "You have not wings for flying. You are not a bird to soar freely through the air, to indulge yourself in the pursuit of beauty. You are a beast of burden, and to eat you must serve your master." Then he saw that he had the legs of a draft horse. He sought in vain for his wings. They were gone. "Alas," he said to himself, "if I have no wings and I cannot fly in the pursuit of beauty, then at least I will eat." He waited for his master's command, and it came in a strange language that he understood only imperfectly. He started off in one direction, but the voice shouted "No!" and a whip came down on his haunches. He listened all the more attentively. Each time he thought he understood, and each time his master said "No!" and the whip came down harder. He never satisfied his master and he never was fed. . . . Then all magically changed, and he was standing outside himself looking at what he was. The horse and the eagle were dead. The beauty was un-viewed, and the food was uneaten. All was confused despair. . . .

The dream of the eagle and the horse haunted Rodion for days. How graphically it presented the plight of the Soviet artist! If only it were possible for him to express it openly. . . .

The urge became an obsession. In some way, he felt, I must say it. . . . And he began to experiment. He knew that if he were to say it he must so disguise his symbolism that its meaning would be clear to only a few, perhaps only to himself—but say it he must. . . .

After several trials he hit on an allegory for children, using the figure of Pegasus, the winged horse of mythology, as the hero. Painstakingly he fashioned a legend in simple but beautiful language. It was the story of the winged horse who had to learn to walk and work. He told of the youthful Pegasus who flew proudly through the skies. One day he was captured by man. Man clipped his wings and harnessed him to the plow. Each day Pegasus would be led out into the fields to till the soil. He would look longingly up at the sky and realize that never more would he fly. The master would give his orders, and Pegasus would obey as best he could. If he obeyed well, the master would reward him with oats; if he did not obey well he would receive curses and blows. When he was too old to be useful, his owner set him free. He tried to fly—but fell to the ground. His long unused wings were no longer capable of supporting him in flight. The birds ridiculed him because he could not fly, and the other horses mocked him because of his wings. He could not decide what he was. . . . "But who is to say?" he concluded. "Am I a bird because I have wings—or am I a horse because I cannot fly? What am I? What am I . . . ?"

The parable was an instantaneous and outstanding success, partly because it had great appeal for children (testimonials from school teachers poured in to the publishers), but mainly because of the critical interpretation that was put on the symbolism.

Rodion Trofimovich read the review in the *Teacher's Gazette* incredulously:

"In the present period of conflict between the democratic world and the western capitalist warmongers one must welcome the appearance of R. T. Letnik's parable, *Pegasus No. 7*. Using as a point of departure the classical legend of the winged horse, R. T. Letnik fashions in clear direct symbolism a representation of the exploitation of the workers in the capitalist countries. The worker is symbolized by Pegasus. Exemplifying the unity of physical and mental work, Pegasus combines in himself the capacity of creative imagination, symbolized by his wings, and of productive labor, symbolized by his horse's body and legs. The capitalist exploiter, seeking to enslave Pegasus, clips his wings and permits the development only of his brute powers. When he has outlived his usefulness, the exploiter casts him aside.

"Depicting in clear and forceful language the manner in which the capitalist system thwarts the many-sided development of the working masses, R. T. Letnik provides a valuable weapon for the political education of future Soviet citizens, arming them with the proper political understanding which will make them creative builders of a new socialist order.

"He is especially to be commended for the simplicity and beauty of his language, and for having fashioned his legend in a form which makes it inherently interesting to children of the primary school.

"The State Pedagogical Publishing House should see to it directly that this volume is made available in sufficient numbers so that it may be accessible to every child in the primary school."

There were equally enthusiastic reviews in *Child and Family,* in *Soviet Pedagogy,* and finally even in the authoritative Party organ, *Culture and Life.*

Rodion was dumbfounded. His dream had brought him both prestige and wealth. An animated cartoon was made for the movies. He was commissioned to convert *Pegasus No. 7* into a play for the children's theatres. A car was put at his disposal by the Writers' Union. He was invited to join the Party, a request which he declined gracefully by pleading that he was presently too occupied with a new novel. His royalties ran over a hundred thousand rubles in the first year.

Rodion basked in fame and wealth—but there were conflicting thoughts in his mind. "Have I fooled the authorities," he asked himself repeatedly, "or have I merely played into their hands? Does anyone beside myself understand the true meaning of my symbolism? Should I laugh—or . . ."

One day he heard that Krotki was back in town. He had been around to one of the theatres looking for work, and had left his address. Surely, Rodion thought, if anyone caught my message, it would be Krotki. . . .

His chauffeur drove him to Krotki's lodging in a poor district. Rodion looked uneasily out at the street. He felt self-conscious in this neighborhood with his European clothes and his Homburg. He hurried into the building, and along the hall to the room at the rear. As he raised his hand to knock, he heard the sound of voices coming from within. One at least seemed to be raised in excited argument. He smiled to himself, and rapped sharply.

The door opened part way and a face peeped out. It was Krotki. As he recognized Rodion, he threw the door wide open. Rodion knew instantly from his friend's appearance that he had been taking part in a literary discussion; his collar was open, his shirt half unbuttoned, and his hair rumpled.

Krotki embraced Rodion and pulled him into the room.

With one hand he made a broad sweeping gesture, taking in the half-dozen figures who sat wreathed in tobacco smoke.

"Rodya, I wish to present to you the members of the Pegasus Literary Circle. It is composed of writers who have resolved never to let their wings grow weak from lack of exercise, even though they may be harnessed to the plow to earn their bread. We welcome you as our most eloquent spokesman."

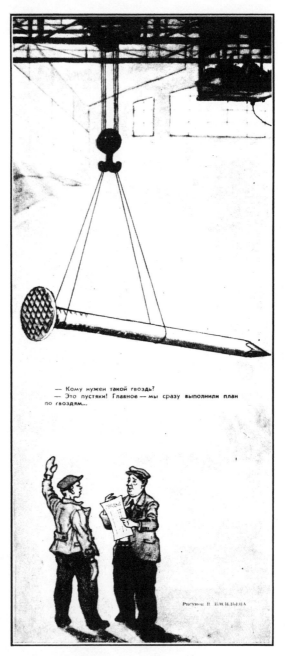

—Who needs a nail as big as that?

—Who cares? The important thing is we fulfilled the plan for nails at one fell swoop.

KROKODIL

The Factory Director

As the story went, a factory director needed a new chief accountant. The applicants were almost all newly out of school and had no job experience. The director asked each the same question: "How much is two and two?" Each answered: "Four," and the director ushered him politely from the office. Finally, an old-timer came in, with many years of experience with Soviet accounting. The same question was put to him. He screwed up his face, looked quizzically at the director and asked: "How many do you need?"

"How many do you need? How many do you need?" Dmitrov repeated ironically to himself as he waited impatiently for his call to the Ministry to go through. The supply chief sat at the opposite side of the desk drawing railroad cars filled with coal on a piece of scrap paper. Dmitrov's secretary came in to say the Ministry was on the phone.

Dmitrov was at his most affable when calling the Ministry for supplies: "Good day, Andrei Grigoreivich. We have a little problem. This month's supply of coal hasn't arrived. . . ."

The supply chief leaned forward, trying to piece in the other end of the conversation.

"Yes, Andrei Grigoreivitch, we realize the Ministry has many plants to supply. . . . No, Andrei Grigoreivitch, we must have twenty carloads by the fifteenth. . . . It's impossible, we can't get along with thirteen, we wouldn't last to the end of the month. . . . Fifteen?" Dmitrov nodded to the supply chief and gave a slight wink. The supply chief drew a big car and put the number 15 in the middle of it. "I don't see how we can do it on fifteen. All right, all right. . . . Good, good, we'll try it if that's all you can spare. But it's going to be close. Thanks. Good-bye."

He hung up and relaxed back into his chair with a smile.

The supply chief crumpled his doodles into a ball and tossed them lazily into the waste basket. "I was afraid you were going to give in at thirteen. Well, with fifteen we'll have about five cars for 'insurance.' "

They shook their heads half sadly and half humorously at the perpetual comedy of asking twice as much as you needed, hoping to get what was necessary.

The supply chief left the office muttering sententiously: "Necessity writes its own laws."

It was late in the afternoon, and the successful call to the Ministry was an ideal note on which to leave the office. Dmitrov stuffed his brief case with papers he wanted to work on that evening, put on his coat, and told his secretary to tell the night superintendent that he could be reached at the dacha throughout the evening. The secretary picked up the phone and called the motor pool to tell his chauffeur that he was leaving the office.

He walked out through the shop. The men caught sight of the familiar figure clad in a business suit and carrying a brief case and they worked a trifle faster, stopped their bantering, and kept their eyes fixed on their machines. Glancing from side to side as he strode through the shop, Dmitrov noticed a man working on a grinding machine without safety glasses. He stopped and gave the man a thorough tongue lacing. Dmitrov called the man's foreman over, and bawled him out for laxity in enforcing safety regulations. He told him that the next man in his section who didn't wear safety glasses while grinding was to be fined a week's pay.

Dmitrov was proud of his factory. He tried to keep it as up-to-date as possible. But sometimes he felt it an endless and thankless task trying to get workmen to use the most elementary of safety precautions. They worked hard but they had a callous indifference to the harm that machinery could do to them. He knew what injuries could do to a production schedule.

He closed the door of the shop behind him, muffling the clatter of the machinery. The chauffeur was waiting. He held the door open as Dmitrov got into the back seat. Closing the door after Dmitrov, he jumped in front and swung the car onto the street out of the plant.

"To the dacha, Comrade Director?" he called over his shoulder.

"Yes."

It was summer, and he had moved his family out of their winter apartment to the cottage in the country.

Dmitrov settled back into his seat and pulled from his brief case the production and stock figures that the chief of the statistical section had dropped on his desk that afternoon. He knew they contained good news, but he was eager to see the details. His finger ran quickly across the page . . . tractor production up 5 percent over the previous month . . . parts up 15 percent! . . . that was a pleasant surprise . . . stocks of steel scrap were a little low . . . that would need attention . . . all in all a very good picture.

The car sped past the fields of a large kolkhoz. Groups of field hands were scattered across the landscape. Some were so close to the road that Dmitrov could see the sweat running down the faces of the women as they worked. Ever so often he would see a tractor pulling a cultivator, doing the work of many field hands. Could they possibly understand the miracle of creating a tractor. . . . He remembered the announcement in the morning newspaper that the wheat harvest in the Raion would exceed last year's record by fifteen percent.

Why? He mused. He answered himself that it was because they had more tractors and more machinery. Next year it would be even better. His plant's production had increased every month for the last four months.

The road took a turn. Suddenly far across the fields through the trees he caught a brief view of his plant, with wisps of smoke trailing across a distant sky pierced by the tall chimneys of the foundry.

A damned good plant, he thought . . . and to have a damned good plant you have to have a damned good director. . . .

Dmitrov leaned back with a feeling of contentment, almost of complacency. These were unusual feelings for him. He was by temperament scarcely a contented and complacent man. But to be a damned good factory director was a matter of pride and satisfaction. . . . To be a successful director of a Soviet factory you have to be on your toes. Crisis is the normal state of affairs. . . . Every job is impossible but you have to make it possible. . . . They hold you to *your* plan but the bastards don't get the material to you. . . . What ever happens to *their* plan? Where does the steel go? Who gets the electric motors that were supposed to go into your cranes? Everybody has a perfectly good explanation . . . but their explanations don't solve your problems . . . will those pompous bureaucrats in the Ministry take *your* explanations? . . . hell, no! . . . it's up to you to get the job done some way or other, and some way or other you do. . . . It's not always legal, and everybody knows it, the Ministry, the Party Organizer, the Raion Committee—everybody . . . but they'll keep their mouth shut if it works . . . it's their neck too . . . but one mistake . . . get caught doing something! . . . or worse yet, don't get the job done! They're down on you with a dossier that will make you look like Leon Trotsky himself. Oh, well, you can't make an omelet without cracking eggs and you can't build socialism without cracking a few skulls. . . . You can't build it either without men who can get out production . . . you're the man they depend on.

It is not *à la mode* for Soviet men of action to write autobiographies. Nevertheless Alexei Mikhailovitch Dmitrov sometimes came close to composing one in moments of reverie such as this. He thought of himself as the exemplification of the new and better type of Soviet factory director, and to some extent he could not help occasionally looking back—with more than a little surprise and wonderment—on the road he had traveled. He was born a little before the Revolution. His social background—not bad— mother a peasant, and father a village school teacher. The family moved to the city during the Civil War. For safety's sake he always recorded his father's occupation as a peasant . . . you never knew . . . whether it was a good idea or not . . . if you got away with it fine . . . but if they found out you would be in a hell of

a mess. . . . He got his engineering training in the early thirties
. . . engineers are the men who build socialism . . . they are
trusted and rewarded . . . you held your breath and covered up
anything in your background that might keep you out of engineering school. . . .

It was a risk, and Dmitrov knew it, to get into the Party and into
engineering school with even a slight falsification of the facts.
But it was a risk worth taking.

Smartest thing I ever did . . . he often told himself . . . sure
the Party is a lot of trouble . . . more meetings to attend . . .
more people barking at you if you slip up . . . but a non-Party
engineer is stuck . . . you'll never get a plant of your own without a Party card.

. . . You didn't join to become director . . . it was more a
symptom of something more basic, that you wanted to become a
director, that you *would* become a director, and that other people
—particularly people in the Party—*knew* that you would be . . .
it was part of a feeling that you wanted to and could become a
director . . . some engineers just aren't cut out to be directors!
. . . they'd rather keep their noses buried in technical problems.
. . . It wasn't political . . . you didn't have to be an activist to
join the Party . . . maybe you even hated Stalin's guts. . . . And
it wasn't your background . . . if you really wanted to join the
Party you could cover up your social background . . . the reason
they didn't join the Party and didn't become factory directors is
that they couldn't stand the pace . . . it takes too much out
of them.

Sometimes he envied the engineers. Dealing with technical
problems is a snap, he thought . . . it's true engineers have their
problems and some share of administration . . . but when you
get down to it, it's the director who has to get things done, who
has his neck out all the time . . . it's like being a juggler with
somebody always throwing in another ball just when you think
you have the situation under control.

. . . like a few years ago . . . the plant was almost back in
shape, reconverted from turning out tanks during the war . . .
one of the first plants reconverted, too . . . then the damned
grain shortages . . . the men hungry, productivity falling off

. . . men absenting themselves to look for grain in the villages . . . those on the job too weak to work well . . . if only you could serve them one good meal a day in the plant cafeteria. . . . The expediter solved that one.

Dmitrov remembered the day the expediter showed up in the office, snapping to attention and delivering a mock salute. His irreverence was irritating but you had to put up with it. Maybe that was part of what made him a good expediter. "Comrade Director, I believe I have found the solution for the alleviation of the acute shortage of grain in the agricultural sector of our economy."

"Fine. I suppose you are prepared to offer me the opportunity of buying it on the black market at ten times the legal rate, and thereby relieve me simultaneously of any concern for what to do with the surplus of cash in the director's fund," Dmitrov snapped and waved the expediter to a seat.

"No, no, Alexei Mikhailovitch. I paid a few social visits to acquaintances of mine in some of the neighboring MTS's. We got to discussing the severe shortage of grain and the equally severe shortage of tractor parts in the same breath. To make a long story short, they have enough grain put away for 'insurance' to make it interesting to us for a few spare parts. With the pressure on for new tractors, nobody's making parts. They're more desperate than we are. So, with your permission, I will instruct the shop chief to 'discover' that an appropriate number of parts are defective and must be scrapped. Then I will, again with your permission, borrow a few trucks from the pool and do my bit to overcome present gross deficiencies in maintaining agricultural machinery in proper socialist working order."

"I'd better talk to the shop chief about having the parts declared scrap," said Dmitrov. "In the meantime don't let that new young Partorg find out how you're getting the grain. If he asks, tell him that the kolkhozniki are making a voluntary contribution out of an awareness of the importance of maintaining production of agricultural machinery at a maximum level. He will understand that kind of language but he's still a little uninformed about the realities of running a factory."

. . . The expediter, how could you ever run a factory without him . . . he seemed to have relatives and friends in the right place to get you out of every possible sort of a jam. . . .

. . . But did the Partorg ever find out how you ever got that grain . . . you never really knew . . . how could you tell what was on his mind when he made his speech at the next meeting of the plant's Party organization . . . it could have meant anything.

He stood up and said: "Alexei Mikhailovitch, I am new in this Raion, but I am truly amazed and, of course, very pleased to observe the extraordinarily high level of political consciousness among the kolkhozniki of this area. It is a fine tribute to the work of the Raikom that the kolkhozniki have voluntarily contributed a portion of their own grain to factory workers. I think we should inform the Raikom of this event."

. . . was he being ironical . . . you couldn't take a chance . . . you had to answer him so that you had him either way. . . .

"I quite agree with you," Dmitrov answered. "It was a rare act of political consciousness on the part of the kolkhozniki, and not a day too soon. We have, as you pointed out, an excellent Raikom, and we have unquestionably benefited from their splendid political work. But remember, Comrade Partorg, that the one thing on which the Raikom is adamant—we have to meet our production quotas. Remember we were twenty percent behind schedule when we got the grain, and production came right up afterward. Yes, I agree we have an excellent Raikom, and they certainly aren't a batch of stuffy bureaucratic bastards. They don't ask *how* you got things done. They just want to make sure that they're done. I must say," and he dropped his voice to the level of a confidential conversation, "I was particularly glad for your sake that the food came through when it did. You know it doesn't look good for a new Partorg if the plant falls behind just when he comes on the job. Of course, we all know the reasons, but sometimes the Raikom and the Ministry get more concerned with the results than the reasons. As I say, I was quite glad for your sake."

The Partorg was silent.

To make sure the lesson stuck, Dmitrov made a point of praising the Partorg to the Raikomsec—in the presence of the Partorg himself, of course—for his fine cooperation, initiative and lack of bureaucratic formalism.   After that the Partorg had to go along with Dmitrov.

. . . not a bad fellow once he learned the facts of life. . . .

. . . but in situations like this sometimes you wonder whether the old Bolshevik directors didn't have it better. . . . Party members, some of whom could scarcely write their names, but got positions of responsibility because they were reliable politically . . . sure you have a better technical training . . . you understand what's going on in the plant, and you don't have to let the chief engineer do the talking for you with the Ministry . . . but when it came to Party matters and influence in the government, the old boys were better off . . . they were Party people first, and technical specialists afterwards—if at all. . . . Take the duffer who ran your plant in 1936 . . . the stories they told about him . . . when an old technical specialist got in trouble with the secret police he went straight to the Central Committee and had him back on the job in a week . . . the big shots were old comrades of his . . . he wouldn't have to handle a smart aleck of a young Partorg with kid gloves. . . .

. . . but on the other hand that's why they weren't around any more . . . the Party couldn't control them . . . very few of them survived the purges of the late thirties . . . and most of those were replaced by younger technicians by the end of the War. . . .

When Dmitrov thought of them they seemed like prehistoric creatures, just as the period of the purges seemed a nightmare to be forgotten if possible.

A young man just out of school, Dmitrov had scarcely known what to make of the purges.   One hero after another fell, some of them the men who had wrought the Revolution, and many of whom had built the Soviet industry of which he was so proud. Men were praised for their faithful service to the Party and the country one day and disappeared the next . . . were they really traitors? . . . if they were, whom could you trust? how could you trust anybody? . . . if they weren't traitors, what was happening? . . . how could you tell an innocent mistake or a difference in judgment from treachery and sabotage. . . .

The effect on the morale of technical personnel was marked.

It was obvious that many of his co-workers were shaken in their faith in the regime. Dmitrov's own doubts never crystallized. He had too much to do! His problems were too immediate and pressing to permit thinking about politics. In quick succession he moved from junior engineer to production engineer. The purges virtually stripped the plant of its older technical and administrative personnel and suddenly he found himself the chief engineer of the factory.

He was only thirty, and already saddled with tremendous responsibilities—which meant tremendous dangers. Dmitrov survived strains which broke other men. He did it by learning to repress his fears and doubts, and by throwing himself into the problems at hand.

. . . any misstep can bring trouble . . . demotion . . . arrest . . . worse. You don't even have to make a mistake . . . just have a wrong friend, or get denounced by someone who is after your scalp . . . or your job.

But, where others froze to inaction, Dmitrov buried himself in the job and refused to think of danger. He developed also the indispensable trait of the successful Soviet executive, a measure of callousness, or obtuseness that permitted him to drive directly ahead, insensitive to minor obstacles, to dangers, and to vexing personal considerations that befuddle, confuse, and inhibit those more given to sentimentalism.

He got his first plant just before the war. The first year of his directorship was not very successful. They filled only eighty percent of the plan. He was plagued by continued rebukes from the Raikom and the Commissariat, and by caustic remarks in the local press. Despite his attempts to repress his fears, Dmitrov broke into a sweat every time he got a telegram from the Commissariat, and he opened it with moist and trembling fingers.

He remembered vividly one terrible morning in Moscow. Summoned to report on the reasons for the lag in production, he went to the Commissariat accompanied by the chief engineer, a non-Party man who had served in the plant since it had been built during the first Five Year Plan.

"What in the name of the devil are you doing out there?" he was asked.

"Perhaps I should explain to the Comrade Commissar that I have been in the plant only two months and—"

"None of your goddamned excuses. Even the saboteur who was in there before you got more production out than you do. What are you doing dragging this lop-eared engineer along with you? Couldn't you learn enough engineering to handle your own problems? I should think—"

"But, Comrade Commissar, I am new at—"

"Dammit, I didn't ask you if you were new at the plant, and no more excuses! Beat it! Get back there and get some tractors out, and don't bring me any more excuses or I'll tell you what you can do with them."

Dmitrov reeled from the office.

As time went on he learned to be prepared for such abuse. It wasn't typical of all men in high places. But still there were many who covered up their own defects by shouting, stamping, pounding the table, and cursing. One had to learn who they were, and occasionally to scream back at them. But that was risky.

After a few sessions like that Dmitrov resolved to meet production schedules no matter what happened. That was the turning point in his career. He found that the Commissariat—after the war the Ministry—and the Party overlooked virtually anything if only he kept production up . . . true, the old type director had his political connections in Moscow . . . but you can hold your production record over their head . . . the director of the largest factory in the Raion is a person of importance to the Party officials . . . their reputations depend on you . . . that's your weapon . . . and so does the Ministry . . . they have to fulfill their plan, too . . . and that means they, too, depend on you . . . and next to actually fulfilling your plan, at least maintain the *appearance* of having filled it . . . a good bookkeeper is a valuable asset . . . two plus two is as much as you need. . . .

The magic symbol of "plan fulfillment" ties people together in a peculiar circle of responsibility, mutual assistance, and of suspicion, distrust, and criminal conspiracy. Dmitrov had known the realities of Soviet life before he became director, but only now did he begin to appreciate the complicated web of relationships and circumstances in which he was to be plunged. He urged the foremen to get more production out of their men. The foremen, to keep the men satisfied, had to falsify work records. He, in turn, shut his eyes to this—knowing that it had to be done even though, if brought into the open, this fact could land him and the foremen in jail. He and the foremen became partners in crime. It happened with the engineers, the supply chief, and the expediter whom he sent scurrying around to locate scarce materials. It happened with the Partorg, the local Party officials, and even the Ministry. Only the naive did not understand the need for illicit devices to achieve the goal of plan fulfillment. Each became involved, if only by shutting his eyes to what happened. Each, in turn, held his breath, hoping that none of the fictions would be unmasked by some outsider, such as an independent Party inspector who was not linked in the same chain of mutual responsibility. Once one thread of the web began to unravel, everyone in the circle of conspiracy was endangered.

It was a delicate bit of judgment to know when to support a fellow conspirator, when to sacrifice him. Dmitrov had to make this decision only twice.

. . . there was the foreman who got drunk and tore into a visiting Party big-shot—told him that there wouldn't be so much spoilage if the blasted bureaucrats would see to it that they got decent machine tools instead of coming around snooping at people who were trying to get some work done . . . he was arrested, and the Secret Section turned up a fat dossier proving he had been falsifying work records.

Dmitrov had to join in denouncing him to save his own skin.

. . . this Secret Section, you never really knew their attitude toward those things . . . maybe they didn't care unless somebody wanted to get you for something else . . . they must know . . .

Or maybe it would get complicated by something political like the case of the supply agent.

Dmitrov needed a truck. It was right during the war. They were harder to get than a copy of the Bible in a state bookstore. The supply agent was full of initiative, but, it turned out, not of discretion.

The supply agent showed up one morning and announced proudly: "The truck, Alexei Mikhailovitch, has been found!"

"Good, where did you get it?"

"I contacted an American engineer who has just finished a re-finery in the K—— region. For a few liberated Leicas, and a brief lecture on the desirability of allied cooperation, he let me drive off with a used Chevrolet."

Dmitrov was furious.

"May you join your mother in hell! You crazy horse's tail. My God, don't you know that those foreign missions are covered? You idiot? There isn't a chance in a hundred that they haven't trailed you back to the plant. God himself knows what they'll make of this business. I'll have to report you, that's all . . . I'll have to report you."

"My God, Comrade Director, don't do that!"

"I can't help it. How could you be so stupid?"

The supply chief got eight years.

Dmitrov learned how to assess the people around him, and he acquired techniques of tactical maneuvering that enabled him to get what he wanted without showing his hand. His life ran on a more even keel and the performance of the factory went up.

The director and the engineers waged an annual battle with the Ministry to keep the plan within bounds so they could fill or overfulfill it. After a few years, Dmitrov realized there were certain elements of sham in this fight—the Ministry was just as anxious as you were to have a little "water" in the plan. If the individual plants didn't fulfill their plans, then the Ministry couldn't fulfill its own. An unspoken conspiracy developed: Dmitrov's task was to present a plausible set of figures, and the Ministry carried out its part by not inspecting these figures too closely.

Such convenient arrangements, however, were disturbed by shifts of personnel in the Ministry, by periodic replacement of Partorgs, by new men who were bent on ferreting out bureaucratic feather-bedding, and by the prying from outside inspectors. It was as if some hand inspired by the devil intervened to stir things up just when you got things stabilized and might begin to enjoy the comforts of security.

Dmitrov's greatest satisfaction was the smooth operation of his plant, and he had his worst fights with the Party and the bureaucracy over this. Somebody was always trying to make a hero out of himself and everybody else by handing you some emergency job that would knock the hell out of the flow of production.

Right after the war, one of these fights gave him his worst scare since the purge. A member of the Oblast Central Committee was sold on a new type of harrow supposed to suit the local soil. He wanted a hundred experimental models turned out. The Oblast Committee approached the Ministry. The Ministry ordered Dmitrov's plant to take on this job—just when production was beginning to run smoothly.

Dmitrov went to the Oblast Committee himself, cornered the Secretary and pounded the table.

"Yo∪ damned bureaucrats have no idea what coordinated production is," he shouted. "I'll have to take two engineers and a dozen draftsmen off to design this goddamned harrow and then tie up a whole shop for three months. I won't have you doing this to *my* plant." Then instantly he thought: *"My* plant—Christ, what a blunder! If he caught that, he'll jump all over me. . . ."

The Secretary froze, and then began very politely: "Oh, I beg your pardon, your lordship. The Party has no intention of interfering in the operation of privately owned enterprises. I had assumed that yours was a state factory." And he launched into a violent lecture. "The Party Committee has noticed for some time that you have a tendency to think less and less of the needs of the Party and the country. Who do you think you are, to set your personal interests ahead of . . . This is the kind of behavior . . . Calls for a re-evaluation of your record . . . You will hear further . . ."

A panic such as he had not felt for years spread over Dmitrov. He forced himself to control his behavior. But nothing could suppress the nausea he felt. For days he waited, working mechanically, scarcely seeing or hearing what went on about him. Then the summons from the Territorial Committee, and four long hours of hell-raising, the threat of an official Party censure, and possible discharge and court action if he didn't get the cultivators out in record time and improve his attitude in the future.

Two days later, the front page of the Oblast Party organ featured an editorial: "Toward the eradication of remnants of capitalism in the consciousness of Soviet factory directors." Dmitrov scanned the editorial several times to see if his name was mentioned specifically. . . . No, thank God! At least they're suspending judgment. . . .

Both he and the chief engineer slept in their offices for a month, getting production of the harrows organized without ruining the plant's regular schedule. For this he had to give the chief engineer and his wife a month at a health resort, paid for out of the director's fund.

. . . you knew only too well, being caught between the Party, the Ministry, and the realities of production could be hell at times. . . . God knows you can't overestimate the contributions of the Party to keeping the plant running . . . when you get in a rough spot, the Partorg often helps to cut a lot of red tape. . . . if you look at it from the standpoint of the country, they do jack up a lot of deadheads and prune away at the ministerial bureaucracy. . . . they act as a sort of spark plug and coordinator of the economy . . . but when you feel the bite . . .

Dmitrov had shifts of mood about being a director. There were good days when he was inclined to look favorably not only on the world, but on himself.

The rewards of being a director were considerable, and he thought with satisfaction of the contrast between himself now and the boy who started out in a village school, worked for a while as a laborer, and finally got the education and training that moved him up the ladder of success.

And his wife—one would scarcely recognize the peasant girl just in from the village that he met in evening school in 1929. Now she was the lady of the town which had grown up around the plant, officiating at meetings, leading campaigns, dressed in the latest Moscow fashions.

Those Moscow fashions! Sometimes he wished he had never heard of them. How his Verushka loved her hairdresser and dressmaker! She would commandeer his car to take her to the dressmaker's and let it stand outside for hours while she had her fittings. That came to an end when he was called over to the Raion Committee Headquarters in an emergency and she had the car. He had to take the truck from the motor pool and suffer the embarrassment of dismounting from the cab of the truck in front of the entire Raion Committee. No one said a thing, but it was clear from the suppressed smiles that they all knew where his car and chauffeur were. That night he and Verushka had a long argument. She kept asking tearfully if he didn't want her to dress as a director's wife should. He replied just as often that it wasn't necessary to tie up the director's automobile all day and shame him in front of the entire Raion Committee just so she could put on airs. After that she used the car only sparingly. But these were minor problems. He was proud of the fact that she had kept up with his change of status, that she did not embarrass him by remaining a dumpy hausfrau as so many wives did. She could entertain guests well, and she was a good mother of the children.

. . . and the children—Vanya in the Institute, and Nadia getting ready to study music at a Leningrad conservatory when she finished the secondary school . . . your own house . . . vacation on the Black Sea every year, the plant's affairs permitting . . . the town officials respect you . . . the workers tremble in your presence . . . you don't have to cool your heels for hours in the reception room of the Moscow bureaucrats. . . .

. . . the building of socialism is a big job, and it's the practical men of industry who are doing it. . . . The country is going places, and it's a good thing to feel that you are one of the key people. . . .

There were other days when his doubts climbed to the surface. A nagging little fear that the day might come when the regime would not value his services so highly. Then the little entries in the dossier, the record they must have of all the cutting of red tape, the illicit devices he had resorted to—precisely the things which made him valuable now—would be used against him. On these days, he treated the head of the Secret Section with extra deference.

Sometimes he was infuriated by the sheer injustice of being held to a production norm when no one would insure him a smooth flow of supplies. In munitions production at least the Party and the Ministry saw to it that you got the material you needed. . . . Political doubts—no, but the stupid indignity of mouthing meaningless slogans no one could believe . . . why build socialism on stupidity and inanity? . . . why not admit our faults? . . . why bring political charges against a man for production failure when he had to work with faulty material? . . . another person exiled because a relative had lived under German occupation; so it went. . . .

Sometimes Dmitrov wondered if it were possible to take it easier, to take fewer chances, to produce less and play safe? He thought of Vasiliev, the director of the local electric station. Vasiliev had had the same job for ten or twelve years now, and probably would never advance very far. He took a safe conservative approach to everything, was more interested in keeping what he had than in getting more. A few directors were like that, but Dmitrov couldn't see himself being that way for very long. Being a director is a risky job under the best of circumstances, so you might as well reap the benefits. . . .

The car lurched as it hit a rut. Dmitrov caught himself on the back of the front seat.

"Be careful," he barked.

"Yes, sir, Comrade Director," answered the chauffeur.

Dmitrov looked at the back of the chauffeur's neck. He seemed a decent enough chap, but they said that every chauffeur reported on his boss to the MVD.

"Goddamn it," shouted Dmitrov, "if you don't learn to drive any better than that I'll see to it that you go back to driving a truck." Might as well put a little fear into him . . . never does any harm. . . .

"Yes, sir, Comrade Director."

Dmitrov looked at the fields speeding by, and suddenly realized that he was half way out to the dacha.

. . . I've been wasting time, he thought. He returned to the papers which had fallen onto his lap . . . we need steel scrap . . . I'll call the Ministry in the morning . . . how much do we need? . . . how much *is* two and two?

He has mechanized

The Tractor Driver

Vadim Pavlovich Goncharov wormed his way out of the railroad carriage and onto the station platform.

"So," he thought, "this is home. . . ." Seven years since he had been mobilized. Four years of service as a tank driver—wounded twice, captured and escaped once, decorated twice. . . . Three years in the occupation forces. . . . And now he was back to pick up his life where he had left it seven years ago. . . .

The ground was covered with the snow from a late March blizzard, and the wind whistled around him as he headed for the small shanty. He hoped his family had gotten his letter and someone would be able to get to the station with a cart.

A tall figure clothed in an enormous coat covered with patches and badly torn came loping across the platform toward him, calling "Vadim, Vadim!" He strained to recognize the figure hurrying toward him. No! It couldn't be! It was his kid brother, Fedya. Vadim dropped his bags and ran to meet him. They embraced each other, pounding violently on one another's back without speaking. Then Vadim grabbed Fedya by the shoulders and stood him off at a distance.

"Well, let's have a look! Big guy, ain't you! What are you now, sixteen? What are you doing? Still going to school?"

"No, I'm a tractorist since last year, just like you were," said Fedya.

Vadim sized him up and clapped him on the shoulder. "Good boy."

"Hey, come on," said Fedya, embarrassedly. "Papa got his brigadier to lend me a horse and cart to come get you. Give me a bag!"

They climbed onto the small cart and huddled up in anticipation of the cold trip of twenty kilometers to the village. The clop of the horse's hooves was matched by a barrage of questions by both brothers. Fedya wanted to hear about Vadim's war experience and life in the West. Vadim wanted to learn what had happened on the kolkhoz. Gradually, by persistence and at the cost of rapid answers to Fedya's inquiries, Vadim got answers to his questions.

Papa and Mama were in good health. The kolkhoz had suffered terribly under the Germans—and from the depredations of the kolkhozniks themselves during the periods when they were free from political control. Most of the cattle that the Germans had not requisitioned had been slaughtered and eaten by the kolkhozniks. Property was in bad repair after the war. Tractors were in terrible condition. Gradually they began to get back on their feet. New tractors came in. Repairs were made. Some of the boys came back from service. Then the famine of 1947. . . .

"We heard rumors about a famine," said Vadim, "but we didn't know whether or not to believe them. You know, it was the same old thing. You would hear that some guy got a letter from home saying that Uncle Sashka had gotten food poisoning just like his wife did, and the guy knew his aunt had died during the big famine in '33. But we didn't know if there was anything in it or not."

"There was plenty to it. Things were in a hell of a shape. We had a new chairman—you remember him, old Fedin?"

"Sure! I know him. He was a brigadier from the other village. He always kept trying to dodge responsible jobs. How the hell did he ever get that job?" asked Vadim incredulously.

"You know how it is. The man we had in right after the war was some fellow who had messed things up in a war plant, and they made him a kolkhoz director as punishment. Well, he was so bad that they yanked him out of that job and put old Fedin in. The Secretary of the Raikom comes tearing over one day, tells this character he's fired, and then tells us we have to have a meeting of the kolkhoz that night to elect a new chairman. Then we heard that we should select Fedin. So elect Fedin we did."

"What kind of a chairman was he?" Vadim asked.

"Not so bad, and not so good. He's a nice old duffer, but he got himself in a lot of trouble with the grain deliveries when the famine hit. By the time the harvest came people were really starting to drop in the fields. So he distributed our share of grain before we made our deliveries to the state and the MTS. The Secretary of the Raikom would have let him get away with it, but some eager beaver from the Obkom was around trying to step up deliveries, and heard about it. So they gave old Fedin hell and put him back out in the fields as a brigadier."

"Who's the chairman now?"

"An outsider named Soskin. The chairman of the MTS is your old brigadier, Skorsky. He came back in '46, and they made him chairman of the MTS. Is he glad to get you back! He just about hasn't any good tractorists—only a bunch of girls who learned how to drive during the war. Say, you won't know the place. We lost a lot of men. Some of 'em died, and some of the others stayed in the city. More than half of the tractorists are girls now, and nearly all the field hands and dairy workers. Most of the boys who came back took jobs in the beet factory in town. There are twice as many girls as fellows in the village."

"So, I suppose you've been having a good time for yourself?" Vadim grinned at his grown-up younger brother.

Fedya blushed. He was not yet used to talking on a man-to-man basis with this brother who was ten years his senior.

"Well, yes," he said. "All you have to do is walk into the barn and the girls fall down in the hay. You should see your friend Sasha. He was going to get married when he came back, but now he says he's going to be a permanent bachelor. He claims he's a valuable piece of socialist property that shouldn't fall into private hands."

"Why, the old bastard!" Vadim hooted. "I'll treat him to a little socialist competition. So he thinks he's going to become a haystack Stakhanovite, does he?"

Fedya's interests got the upper hand again. He began to ply Vadim with questions about the West. Was it true that the poor people lived much better there? How was the food?

Even with his kid brother Vadim hesitated. The briefing he had gotten on being discharged was fresh in his mind, as were also all the rumors of what happened to soldiers who talked too freely in comparing life in the Soviet Union with conditions in the West. But gradually he relaxed and told Fedya frankly of the enormous contrast between their way of life and the way of life of the capitalist countries.

Fedya was silent, listening without comment.

Vadim changed the subject to the safer matters of local gossip. But now the cold was penetrating through their clothing and into their bones. They were losing their appetite for talk, and huddled shivering on the cart.

"I wish I had some of Auntie Anna's liquid fire," Vadim chattered at one point. "Is she still making it?"

"Up to last year, and then her big pot got a hole in it, and she couldn't get it mended."

Finally the gates of the kolkhoz came in sight, and the familiar sign, "Kalinin #3." They drove past the other village on the kolkhoz and another three kilometers to their own. Most of the kolkhozniks were working indoors, repairing equipment, getting ready for the spring sowing, or tending animals. Occasionally the brothers passed someone on the road. Many of them Vadim recognized and waved to. The younger ones he frequently failed to recognize until Fedya identified them.

At last they rounded a grove of trees and their home village came in sight. Fedya whipped the horse into a gallop, a bit of impetuousness that they both quickly regretted as Fedya tried in vain to avoid the potholes in the road. They both grabbed the reins and pulled the horse back to a walk.

"Phew, Fedya, I'm glad to be home," said Vadim, "but let's not get sent up for destroying socialist property before I get my bags unpacked."

As they approached the small thatched hut in which the family lived, Fedya let out a loud whoop, and their mother came bursting through the door to meet them. There she was, mamushka, a little older, a little rounder, but the same familiar old lady with heavy felt boots, a shawl, and an apron flying in the breeze as she rushed out to meet him.

Vadim jumped off the cart and ran to meet her. She hugged him with tears running down her cheeks. They walked into the hut, with Fedya following, carrying Vadim's two bags as though they were toys.

Vadim stepped past the door and looked at the large room that was the center of the family's living quarters. He peeked into the small second room in which he and Fedya used to sleep. Sure enough, there was his cot, neatly made up, with two carefully patched blankets folded across the foot. . . . His first flush of warmth at being home was offset by the contrast with the homes of German peasants he had seen. God, he thought, if they only knew the difference. . . .

"Where's Papa?" he asked.

"Over in the calf barn," Mama answered. "They're whitewashing it this week. He'll be home around seven o'clock for dinner. But we have to go to a meeting at the clubhouse tonight. They're announcing the plans for spring sowing. If this snow clears away we'll start in a couple of weeks."

"Oh, hell," thought Vadim, "the first evening I'm home, and everybody's tied up in a damn meeting. . . ."

Fedya sensed his feelings and said: "Look, Vadim, why don't you come over to the meeting later? A lot of the boys from the MTS are coming over with their instruments and we're going to have dancing after the meeting."

Papa came home around seven. Like Mama, he looked much the same, but older. He walked with an air of weariness and resignation that was new to Vadim.

They had an enormous supper preceded by a few discreet toasts with vodka that Papa produced from a corner in his side of the room. Vadim had been itching for a good slug of vodka since he got off the train. What was a celebration without a good stiff drink? He wished the old man were more generous with his liquor.

After dinner the old folks went off to the kolkhoz meeting, leaving Fedya and Vadim to themselves.

"When are the boys going over?" Vadim asked.

"Oh, around ten o'clock. The meeting should be over by about that time."

Vadim fished around in his pockets and pulled out several crumpled ruble notes. "Do you suppose you could promote a bottle of vodka for a little celebration?"

"Forget it," answered Fedya. "I think the boys will have plenty. Sasha had a lot of kerosene stored up from last fall, and one of the boys went into town to trade it for some liquor this morning."

"Sounds like old times," said Vadim, "trading kerosene for vodka. How's the kerosene norm now?"

"I guess just about like before the war. The year before last we had a hell of a time. We had to plow while the ground was still hard, and I lost my shirt. I went over my norm and got docked for the first three pay periods. But last year was a honey. The ground was soft, and the brigadier took it easy on us. Some of the older drivers taught me how to fudge on the turns and to plow shallow. So I made out good."

"You're lucky old Skorsky is chairman. The guy who had the job before Skorsky was a terror, but Skorsky used to give us a break. We'd be plowing on some kolkhoz and the kolkhoz chairman would come around with a stick measuring how deep the cuts were. Then the next thing you'd know he'd have the chairman of the MTS over raising hell with Skorsky, and Skorsky would look at the cuts as though he was the most surprised guy in the world. He'd shake his head and say: 'Yeh, the cuts are too shallow. I keep tellin' 'em to plow deeper. Well, I'll tell 'em again.' Then he'd come over to us and tell us to take it easy until we moved on to the next kolkhoz."

"Did he have you guys plow over his private plot?"

"Sure, but so did everybody else. Hey, how about going over to the meeting now? Isn't it about time?"

They slipped into their coats and walked the three kilometers back to the other village. Being the larger of the two villages on the kolkhoz, and closer to the main road, it contained all the official buildings.

As they approached the large lighted building, they saw a few figures approaching from various directions. They were men and girls who worked on the regional Machine Tractor Station and lived in these or other villages. Like Fedya and Vadim, they were coming for the dancing. Fedya and Vadim slipped into the hall and stood in the back waiting for the meeting to end.

Vadim needed no one to tell him what had been going on. On the platform in front of the hall were the big shots: The Raion Secretary, the members of the Raion Committee of the Party, the chairman of the Village Soviet, the chairman of the kolkhoz, the agronomist, and the chief of the construction brigade. He knew what had gone before: The Raion Secretary had given a pep talk, and discussed the new season in agriculture in terms of the country's economic needs; then the kolkhoz chairman presented the plan for the kolkhoz for the next year. It looked to Vadim, from the glum appearance of the peasants and the vehemence of the Secretary's concluding address, that the news had been bad. Vadim was glad that he was going back to work on the MTS.

No matter how you figure it, he thought, these guys get the worst of it. The ministry tells 'em how much they have to deliver to the state. The MTS takes its cut regardless of anything. Then the kolkhoz takes what's left. No wonder the kolkhoznik wants to spend all the time possible working on his own little plot. That's the only way he can be sure of what he's going to get. . . .

The speech came to an end, and the older peasants left silently. They were carefully holding their tongues until they got off by themselves away from possible informers. One could see that many couples were going to lie awake in bed that night, whispering quietly if there were children in the house, complaining loudly if no one could overhear them.

A few of the younger people began shifting the chairs back against the wall. Vadim went to join them, but as he moved across the center of the floor he met one after another of his old friends, and some of the girls he had known. A circle formed around him. Most of the young men were married. Sasha stood there grinning in front of Vadim—boots polished, a clean shirt, a real dandy.

Sasha plucked Vadim out of the group and pummeled him on

the back. He led Vadim over into a corner, where he gave him a drink of vodka and a long briefing on the women in the villages. Sasha recommended the widows, three of whom had their own huts. They had given up hope that anyone would want to marry them and support their children—so they were always good for a lot of fun.

The music started up and the dancing began. As Vadim saw the large number of girls dancing with each other, he realized how much the girls outnumbered the boys in the hall.

"Sasha," he asked, "are there that many widows?"

"Not entirely, Vadim. A lot of the boys have gone into town to work. But mostly it's from the boys getting killed off in the war."

As the vodka took hold, Vadim's spirits rose, and he and Sasha began to dance. Vadim danced first with some of the girls his own age, girls he had known before the war. As he got a closer look at them he was shocked to see how they had aged. Girls twenty-eight or twenty-nine looked to be forty. Their faces were rough and lined. Their clothing was old and mended. They came to dance carrying a pair of good shoes in a paper bag and changed inside the door. The German farm women he had seen in the villages had looked much younger and had been far better dressed.

Vadim began dancing with the younger girls. They were no better dressed, but at least they were prettier and livelier. Sasha sneaked over and warned him that if he kept hanging around with the younger girls they would have him married the first thing he knew.

As the dancers began to thin out, Vadim began looking for Fedya to go home with him. Fedya had disappeared, however—probably with the tall girl he had been dancing with most of the evening. By this time Vadim was beginning to feel the fatigue of his four-day rail trip, despite the generous use he had made of Sasha's vodka. He declined Sasha's invitation to "fix him up" with one of the girls, and walked home alone.

He slipped quietly into his bed and fell immediately to sleep. Fedya disturbed him only slightly when he came in some hours later.

The household got up at dawn the next morning, gulped down several cups of tea, ate a few pieces of bread, and each went about his business.

Fedya had to repair tractors. He had promised his brigadier to put in overtime to make up for the time he took off to pick up Vadim. Papa was back at his whitewashing job. Mamushka was off tending to the cows.

Vadim took his time, and walked to MTS headquarters toward the end of the morning. The administrative offices were still in the same old frame building. There were the same old sheds for the tractors, but a new repair shed had been built. Vadim walked into the office and looked around. The personnel was all new except for the bookkeeper, a nearsighted old man who used to be a tradesman in town. He should properly have belonged to the expropriated groups, but when collectivization came he possessed a rare and valuable skill: he could keep accounts. So there he was still! He glanced up at Vadim without recognizing him.

Vadim looked about. There were three stenographers and a couple of girls he couldn't place. He asked for the chairman. One of the girls looked up and said he was out in the tractor repair shed. Vadim left and headed for the shed.

As he neared the shed he heard a familiar voice raised to an unfamiliar pitch—Skorsky, ranting and raving. Vadim pushed open the door and looked inside. The shed was packed with tractors, a new type unfamiliar to him. They must be the new, postwar, Soviet type, he realized. The burden of Skorsky's complaint was clear. Half of the station's tractors were out of order. The tractorists were green at repairing. He was blaming the brigadier in charge of the repair section, but it was obvious that most of what was wrong was outside the brigadier's control. . . .

When Skorsky turned away from the brigadier, he saw Vadim standing in the doorway.

"Well, Goncharov, so you're back," he said. "I hope you're coming to work."

Vadim noticed the use of his last name. So Skorsky had slipped into the last-name habit along with all the other bosses. Well, best to follow his lead. . . .

"Well, Comrade Skorsky, I was considering it. Could we have a little talk?"

"Sure. Come on into my office."

Skorsky briefly reviewed the work norms and the wages for tractorists. "Not too good, but better than working in the fields, anyway," he concluded.

"I know, Comrade Skorsky. That's why I learned to drive a tractor in the first place. But I hoped maybe there might be a brigadier's job for me."

"Not now, Goncharov, but maybe by the time summer rolls around. We have only a few old-timers left, and maybe there'll be an opening. We've gotten a lot of girls in the last few years. With the men away, every girl who could struggle her way through four years of schooling asked to be trained as a tractorist. You should see them on repairs—and we have more repairs than ever."

"What's the trouble? Are the old tractors wearing out?"

"Hell, no, some of the oldest tractors are in fine shape. It's the damned new ones that are always falling to pieces." Skorsky stopped suddenly and flushed. He quickly shifted to a new subject.

Vadim was at first puzzled by Skorsky's change of subject, then realized what had happened. The older tractors were American products, and the newer ones were Soviet-made. Skorsky was afraid he might be accused of comparing Soviet production unfavorably with American production. . . .

Vadim agreed to come to work at the beginning of the next week. He still had some money left, and thought he might as well take it easy for a few days.

On the following Monday he came to work, and soon he was back in the routine of the job. He saw quickly that both the materials and the workmanship on the new tractors were poor—not only in comparison with American tractors, but also in comparison with the tanks he had driven and repaired. He knew he would hate to have to fight with one of them.

Repair work continued fairly well, but there was a shortage of parts. Vadim worked hard, even though he took time off to joke with the girls. Skorsky came around from time to time, and often pulled Vadim aside in conversation. It seemed as though he were trying to feel Vadim out on something. At first Vadim suspected he might be trying to provoke him into some indiscreet remark, but after the third or fourth talk it seemed clear that Skorsky had something on his mind, and that he was merely trying to satisfy himself whether or not he could trust Vadim.

One day he called Vadim over to look at a tractor that was standing in the far corner of a shed. "Look, Vadim Pavlovich," he said, dropping into the more familiar form of address, "I have a little job to be done. I know you from before the war, and I think I can trust you to keep your mouth shut. We're short on some materials, and I have some wheat stored up that we didn't sell last fall. What we want you to do is take somebody, maybe that kid brother of yours, and take a wagonload of wheat to the city. I'll get you all the credentials for selling it on the open market, but try to locate some workmen who can supply you with what you need. Don't ask questions. Just get the stuff."

"Okay, I get it," Vadim said. "Just leave it to me."

The next day he and Fedya went to the city. They spent a week there and managed to get most of the material and parts that were needed. By a little adroit managing they succeeded in procuring a secondhand civilian suit for Vadim and a sturdy pair of shoes for Fedya.

Skorsky was delighted with the results and asked no questions about the new shoes and suit. With the proceeds of Vadim's trip they were able to complete their repairs.

Spring was on them, and the life of the MTS and kolkhozes took on the regular swing. The tractor brigades went from kolkhoz to kolkhoz, plowing for spring sowing. Vadim worked from sunup until seven or eight in the evening, and then continued on into the night if there were repairs to be made. He came home night after night dead tired. He saw the family only at the very end of the day. Mamushka and Papa and Fedya were on the same sort of schedule. If anything, the old folks worked harder than their sons. Vadim saw them occasionally in the fields as he rode by on the tractor. Papa was on the repair brigade—mending fences, repairing roads, clearing away brush, doing all the dirty work of the kolkhoz.   Mamushka was out in the fields with the cattle, tending them, feeding them, milking them.

Hard work was bad enough, but Vadim had a harder time getting used to the diet of the kolkhoz.   Even though the fare of a soldier had been sometimes meagre, he had forgotten how sparse and monotonous was the everyday food of a peasant.   The money which he and Fedya brought home helped to raise the family's standard of living above average.   But money, he was reminded, didn't help you buy goods that weren't in the stores. . . . Cloth, which had been scarce but obtainable in German stores, couldn't be bought in the village or even in the adjacent town.   Only a few of the "responsible workers" who were also members of the Komsomol or the Party were able to get cloth with which to make new clothing.   Vadim often thought bitterly of the aspirations of some of the city lads he had been in service with.   If they only knew what rural life was like—the way in which the life of the kolkhoznik was focused on the rawest problems of sheer subsistence.   Thank God, he had at least a little better income and the prestige and satisfaction of operating a tractor. . . .

He seriously considered leaving and going to the city, but then he became interested in one of Sasha's widows—Sonia Ivanovna. Sonia had married one of the village lads, Vladimir Sokolov, early in the war.   She moved in with his family after he left for the front, and bore him a son about three months after he left.   Vladimir was killed.   His father was carried off by the Germans.   Sonia, her son, and her mother-in-law now lived in the two-room hut. Sonia was a passionate girl, but she had been very discreet.   She slept by herself in the small room off the large one in which her son and mother-in-law slept.   Vadim would whistle softly as he walked by the hut on his way back from the repair shed in the evenings, and she would slip out and join him on the bank of the river about seventy-five meters from the hut.

Here, reflected Vadim, is at least one Soviet product that is not inferior to what they have in the West. . . .

There was some humor in kolkhoz life.   In May the village store, for some reason which no one could understand, received a large shipment of surplus military maps.   The women suddenly began buying them in large numbers.   Some enterprising reporter on the Raion newspaper did a story on "Thirst for Culture on the Part of the Kolkhoz Women." He then came around to interview the bucolic lovers of geography—but left the village embarrassed. He found that the women were buying the maps for the cloth backing on which they were mounted. The "cultural side" of the maps was being soaked off in the horse troughs.

The newspaper furnished further amusement a few weeks later. Sasha made the headlines one day. He became a "shock worker" for having plowed ten hectares of ground. Everybody was amazed. Nobody had ever done over six and a half. Sasha should have been equally amazed, but he took his heroism with straight-faced seriousness, and accepted the felicitations of the Partorg with tremendous grace at the next meeting of the MTS. But bit by bit the story of Sasha's success leaked out. A green account-keeper, a young girl just out of school, had made a mistake. Sasha had actually plowed five hectares, but she counted them twice, and so he was credited with ten for the day. The Partorg had been checking over the work records, and passed the story to the newspaper. Later, when they found out the mistake, everybody was embarrassed; but nobody dared to correct it. Sasha was a hero of socialist labor, and there was nothing to be done about it.

The newspapers were a constant joke. Every day at noon one of the school teachers came into the fields to read the paper to the workers while they ate their lunch. They listened to the news with varying degrees of skepticism, trying to read between the lines or to find some verification for the rumors that frequently swept across the kolkhoz. When the teacher finished, there was always a rush for the paper. It was valued more as a source of cigarette wrappings than as a source of news.

Vadim and Sasha had a standard joke. One would say, "I'm thinking of subscribing to the newspaper." The other would ask: "Which one?" And then the first would reply: "Oh, it's all the same to me. Which one has the thinnest paper?" Then they would break into laughter.

Vadim had had his fill of politics in the army. He now wished the Party would let him alone. Even when he left the hut in the morning and walked through the village the loud-speaker which hung from the pole on the street was already blaring forth the theme song of Radio Moscow. A soprano was giving a militant version of "My Moscow" to the accompaniment of a brass band. As they passed out of the village he could hear, dying behind him, the announcements of tremendous successes on the industrial front, of Anglo-American aggression, and of events in the "people's democracies."

Occasionally he satisfied some of his curiosity for what was going on in the West by dropping in on the agronomist, who had a short-wave set. They were old schoolmates and trusted each other enough to listen together to western broadcasts. There was no official ban on such listening—but everyone knew what the Party thought about it; and one did not have to break a law in order to find oneself in trouble. So when Vadim heard something particularly interesting, he managed to pass it on to the other tractorists, or to some of his friends among the kolkhozniks by saying: "I heard a most stupid and unbelievable story over the Voice of America last night." He would then relate it, and always conclude, "Of course, nobody would believe a lot of rubbish like that"—protecting himself in case anyone reported him.

Skorsky brought up again the question of a brigadier's job. He told Vadim it might be easier if Vadim would join the Party. "The Raion Secretary is always trying to push the Party boys, you know," he said.

Vadim shrugged his shoulders. "What do I want to join the Party for?" he demanded. "I've got enough to do as it is. I don't want to go to any more meetings than I have to. I'm not interested in politics. If I can't get to be a brigadier without that, the hell with it."

Skorsky shrugged in return. "Well, I'll see what I can do for you," he said. "But I think you're making a mistake."

Vadim stuck to his guns. He had had enough politics. Somebody was always trying to pump him about the West. "Is it true that the standard of living among the workers in the West is very bad?" "Do the capitalists want war?" he was asked. Vadim kept his mouth shut. You never know when someone will turn out to be a provocateur, he reminded himself. . . . Only with such intimates as Sasha did he talk freely. More than one ex-soldier, he found out, had ended up in a forced labor camp for expressing his opinions. . . .

As summer went on, Vadim became more and more restless. The old folks were boring. They scolded him for drinking. They learned about Sonia, and his father began lecturing about that. His mother was constantly trying to persuade him to give her kerosene to store up for heating in the winter. Sonia wanted to get married. The whole village suspected what was going on between them, and now her mother-in-law was nagging her.

What should he do? He could go into the city and get a good job in a factory. After all, he knew machinery. . . .

He decided to talk it over with Sasha, who, irresponsible as he was, could be sensible enough at times. He invited Sasha to go fishing with him one Sunday, and told him what was on his mind.

Sasha sat for a while, dangling his line in the water under an overhanging branch. "You know, Vadim," he finally said, "I guess we all felt that way when we came back. It was worse when I got out of service. You know by now the shape the farms were in, and how our equipment was shot. . . . I know you're spoilt by the goods you could get in Germany. But believe me, it's much better than it was a couple of years ago. And what good will it do you to go to the city? Nine times out of ten we eat better than they do. If you have to work in a factory, get a job at the beet factory in town. You can stay with your folks and ride in on the bus."

"Well, even if I stay, I don't know what to do about Sonia."

"Why don't you marry her?"

Vadim looked incredulously at Sasha. "What's happened, Sasha? Have you forgotten your principles?" he asked.

Sasha smiled sourly. "I don't know about my principles," he said. "It looks like the whole crew of us have a tough time settling down. Maybe the best thing to do is to decide once and for all to do it, and get the whole matter over with. After all, death and one's wife are ordained by God."

Vadim promised to think about Sasha's advice. But he remained as undecided as ever. He stayed, he figured, because it took less effort to stay than to move. . . .

Then Skorsky called him in one day.

"How about it?" Skorsky asked. "Would you like to be brigadier of the repair section?"

"I suppose so," answered Vadim.

"You suppose!" Skorsky exclaimed. "Maybe if that's all you have to say we should ask one of the young ladies to take over. At least they'd have some enthusiasm. Anyway, you can take over tomorrow morning. And let's see you keep these machines in good shape." He held out his hand, wished Vadim good luck, and said good-bye.

Vadim enjoyed his increased prestige and the additional wages. The work went as well as could be expected.

A few months later Sonia's mother-in-law died suddenly.

Vadim visited Sonia more openly. He got better acquainted with her son, now a boy of eight years. On his days off he took the boy fishing. Occasionally he neglected to come home overnight, and then his mother gave him long lectures on morals. Finally he picked up his things and moved in with Sonia, and they registered their marriage.

He settled down into his way of life completely. Sonia would head off for the fields in the mornings. Vadim and the boy would start down the road.

The loud-speaker would blare out news about the triumph of the people's armies in Korea. The boy would turn to Vadim and ask him about his war experiences. They would continue on in the direction of the school, with Vadim regaling the boy with stories of the conquest of the Fascist beasts.

Vadim's reasoning was simple—if the kid has to grow up and make a living he might as well not worry his head about politics. Let him accept what they told him in school and over the radio. He'd have enough trouble earning a living. . . . "Learn a specialty"—that was the motto Vadim drilled into the boy. Learn some valued skill. Get an education. That's the way to get ahead. . . .

For himself, Vadim took the world as it came. Once in a while he and Sasha would get off for an evening with a pair of Sasha's widows and a bottle of vodka. Sometimes he wondered if he should have moved into the city. Sometimes he wondered what had happened to his friends who had deserted and remained in Germany. But, in the main, he did very little wondering. He was too occupied with the business of keeping the family alive and himself out of trouble. . . .

The Secret Police Agent

Sergei looked about the room at the debris. They had emptied all the drawers, broken half the dishes, smashed the lamp, kicked a hole in the gramophone horn, and strewn clothing about. His mother lay sobbing on the floor, her head pointing toward the open door through which they had dragged his father, stubbornly protesting his innocence, refusing to walk on his own feet. Sergei wiped the tears from his eyes, reached over to his mother and said, half to her and half to himself: "Don't worry, Mama, it's just a mistake, he will be back." She did not answer.

He cried to himself, "It's a mistake! It's a mistake! He will be back! Nothing will happen to us! Somebody made a mistake! They will find out and make it right! . . . That's what I'll tell them at school. . . . It's a mistake, my father is innocent, and I am loyal to the regime. . . ." The words kept ringing over and over in his head: everything will be all right!

At the end of half an hour his mother got up from the floor. She spoke for the first time since the NKVD man had struck her when she protested because they were tearing things apart looking for evidence of his father's "counter-revolutionary activities." Her voice had the thickness that comes from speaking through badly swollen lips. She told him that she was going across town to his aunt's to see if his uncle had any influence. Sergei should wait at the house.

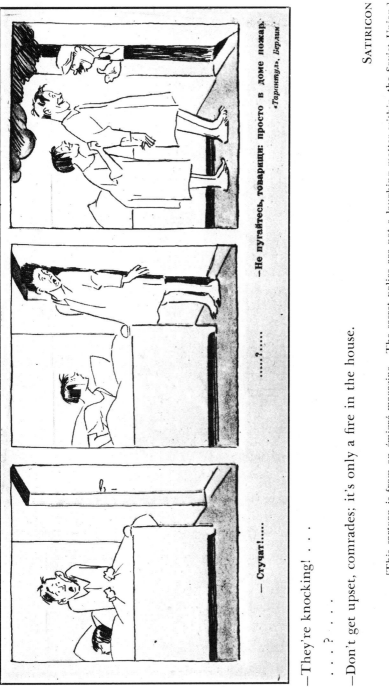

—They're knocking! . . . .

. . . ? . . . .

—Don't get upset, comrades; it's only a fire in the house.

—Стучат!.....

.....?.....

—Не пугайтесь, товарищи: просто в доме пожар.

«Таринтул», Верлин

SATIRICON

[This cartoon is from an émigré magazine. The secret police are not a laughing matter within the Soviet Union.]

She left. He waited until dawn came, frightened, worried, wondering what would happen. The alarm clock kept him company, ticking away in the pile of clothing into which it had fallen. After daybreak he began to wonder what time it was, and he fished the clock out to look at it. Six o'clock! Hours before she would be back. Hours before school began. . . . He waited. Eight o'clock, nine o'clock. School had started. How would he explain being late? . . . Ten o'clock. Maybe she would never come back. . . . Ten-thirty. What will I tell them at school? I'd better go now. Tell them my mother was sick, and I had to go for the doctor, or should I tell them what happened and fight it out?

He took his books and started off for school. The best thing to do was to fight it out. They would surely find out in a matter of days that his father had been arrested. . . .

He came into the front door of the Institute just as classes were changing. He saw Kolya, the Komsomol secretary. "Hi, Kolya." Kolya passed him by without speaking. Sergei grew cold with fright. Yes, they were all passing him by. . . . He walked faster and faster until he came in sight of the wall newspaper. The small group which was reading the morning's bulletin buzzed as he drew up, and then melted away silently, leaving him to himself in front of the newspaper. There it was. They knew already.

AN ENEMY OF THE REGIME

The son of an enemy of the regime cannot be tolerated in our school or in the Komsomol. The father of Sergei Markarych Kazetsky, a student in the first year, has been arrested under section . . . of Article 58 of the criminal code for counter-revolutionary activity. This action of the NKVD, the guardians of our country's safety, should set the pattern for us. The son of such a man has no place in a technical institute training engineers for positions of the highest responsibility in the building of socialism. Nor can he be permitted to remain as a member of the Komsomol. Complete Party vigilance must be exercised in rooting out these and other dangerous elements in our midst.

Expelled from the Institute, from the Komsomol! What would happen to his career as an engineer? . . . He was so overwhelmed with grief and confusion that the events of the day passed mechanically. It was as though he had fallen into such depths of despair that he could neither raise a finger to stem the tide of disaster, nor could additional misfortune add perceptibly to his grief. He was summoned to the Director's office—the Director, an old friend of his father's—and told sternly that he was expelled from the Institute. A special meeting of the Komsomol was called. He sat in stunned silence listening to himself denounced. Some of the more pliable of his friends even joined in the chorus for fear that their association with him might reflect badly on themselves. He did not blame them. He did not blame the Komsomol Secretary. He did not blame the Director. Someone had made a mistake. What could he do about it?

At home his mother and aunt were waiting for him. His mother had been to NKVD headquarters. She could find out nothing. They had taken her passport and stamped it invalid for residence within 100 kilometers of any of the five major cities of the country. They would have to leave immediately for grandfather's place in the village.

They heard nothing of his father's case. But Sergei was concerned more with his own fate than with that of his father. As soon as they arrived in the village, he secured paper and pencil and began writing feverishly, to Stalin, to Kalinin, to the Regional NKVD headquarters, to the Regional Komsomol headquarters, to the All-Union Komsomol, to any official organization he could think of, in the hope of regaining admittance to the Institute. Week after week he waited, receiving no reply.

His mother and he grew apart rather than together in grief. She was forced to work on the kolkhoz in order to support them. His concern with his own welfare filled her with a certain disgust. But she had come to expect such behavior of her menfolks. How could they be such egoists? Imagine a seventeen-year-old boy, so indifferent to his father's fate, so intent on his own interest! Why couldn't he earn some money? The kolkhoz office could use that energy he put into writing letters. . . .

A few form letters arrived, stating that Sergei's petition had been received, and that "it has been forwarded to the proper authorities." His heart sank. Surely nothing would happen! But one day another such official envelope arrived. He tore it open eagerly. From the Kharkov NKVD, from the Regional Office: "If you wish to pursue further the matter discussed in your petition, report with this letter to Lt. Petrov, this office, on the morning of June 17th." No more.

His mother told him that she could not give him the money for the trip to Kharkov, that he would have to get there on his own resources. He promoted several chickens from the neighboring kolkhoz one night and with the money bought a ticket to Kharkov, where he arrived on the evening of June 16th. He spent the night sleeping on the bench in the waiting room. In the morning he washed up in the washroom, smoothing down his hair with his hands, straightened out his shirt collar dirtied by two days' travel, and set out for NKVD headquarters.

What is it like, the NKVD? His mind raced out of control as he walked through town in the direction of the building. . . . It really wasn't something you thought much about, but on the other hand you thought about it a good deal. You were a loyal citizen and you assumed that it was there to protect the country, that the agents of the NKVD were fair and honest, that you had nothing to fear from them. But you heard so many stories! And they *could* make mistakes! And who could be sure whether he himself were guilty or innocent? To what extent can they read into your soul and learn that which you have hidden from yourself?

His step quickened, and his heart sped to keep pace with it. He held his papers in his hand so that he could be sure where they were, so that in his excitement he would not fumble blindly through his pockets and not find them. His hands were perspiring, and the papers were getting wet. He wiped his other hand on his trousers, and shifted the papers.

"They will think I am guilty, and they won't let me back into school. . . . How can I keep from shaking, how can I keep my voice from quivering? By knowing just what I am going to say, that is how. . . ." And he rehearsed block after block as he walked through the city—his autobiography, the facts of his father's arrest—"I knew nothing of his activities," his own desire to become an engineer. "Stalin says that the son should not suffer for the deeds of the father" . . . and there it was, NKVD headquarters.

He scarcely saw the entirety of the façade. His gaze focused on the sign over the entrance, printed in Russian and Ukrainian, "Entrance Strictly Forbidden to Unauthorized Persons." He looked up the long flight of dirty grey steps. He was forcing himself physically to step into a new and unknown world.

At the head of the steps, just inside the entrance doors, was a uniformed guard seated at a desk. Best to sound self-confident and business-like.

"Lieutenant Petrov," he said, trying to produce a smile that would indicate he was at ease but still would not seem too ingratiating. "I have this letter from him."

The guard looked up at him, then down at the letter. "Your passport," he said in a flat, toneless voice.

Sergei handed it to him. The guard looked again at him, and then at the passport. He made a beckoning gesture with his hand above his head. Another guard appeared, and Sergei noticed for the first time that they were stationed every twenty feet or so along the corridor. The guard picked up his papers and motioned Sergei to follow him.

They walked briskly along the corridor. Suddenly the guard stopped and rapped quietly on one of the doors leading off the corridor. A muffled "Enter" came from the other side. The guard opened the door, stepped aside to let Sergei enter. He followed Sergei into the room and handed the papers to the officer who sat writing at the desk in the center of the office.

The officer looked through them. "Uh-huh, citizen Kazetsky, sit down." He went over to a filing cabinet and pulled out a folder which he opened on the desk in front of him. Then he turned to Sergei and smiled. He had a bland, characterless face which seemed to be able to register any emotion that its owner thought necessary. "You would like us to help you?"

"Yes, sir."

"We are very well acquainted with your case." (How familiar those words were to become.) "Now I would like to ask you a few questions. There is no use in hiding anything from me. It will be better for you if you are completely frank and admit everything." (Admit it, Sergei, whether you did it or not!) "Now I understand completely that you are a loyal citizen. . . ."

"Yes, Lieutenant Petrov, I am of course completely loyal."

"Then begin by telling me why you did not report your father's treachery to us."

Then began an hour of questioning and cross-questioning in which Sergei explained in detail, time after time, that he knew nothing about treachery on his father's part. "I am a loyal citizen, Lieutenant Petrov. If I had known at any time of treachery on the part of my father I would have reported it faithfully to the NKVD. After all, I am a faithful member of the Komsomol. We have held up to us continuously the example of Pavlik Morozov, who did not hesitate to report his father when he found his father to be a traitor to the Bolshevik order."

"Yes, yes, I understand. Then you disassociate yourself completely from your father's treachery?"

"Yes, of course, Lieutenant Petrov." My God, I didn't mean to say that. Well, what difference does it make, if they are going to hold him guilty they will anyway. Might as well save myself. . . .

"Good, now you know that we are very anxious to help you. All we want you to do is to return to the Institute. And, of course, as a loyal Soviet citizen you will naturally cooperate with us. Now we have reason to believe that . . ."

No! This isn't what I bargained for—to be an agent, to be an informer, to be a lone wolf whose hand is turned against every man's. . . . I can't back out now. If I say no, then everything will be lost. I'll have to go along for the moment. Maybe I'll find a way out later. One thing at a time, Sergei. . . .

"Naturally, Lieutenant Petrov, as you said, I am anxious to be of any service I can. You know that I am a loyal citizen, and was a member of the Komsomol. I would not want to return to school if I could not return to membership in the Komsomol. I hope that you will be able to explain to the Komsomol authorities that I am completely loyal, and aid me in reentering the Komsomol."

"You must understand that I can exercise no direct influence on the Komsomol authorities," Lieutenant Petrov said firmly.

Sergei interrupted passionately: "If I cannot return to the Komsomol, then I do not want to return to school. Forget the whole matter."

For the first time in the conversation Lieutenant Petrov seemed to be genuinely pleased with Sergei. This pleasure was not expressed directly, but took the form of a suppressed smile and a slightly warmer tone of voice. "Very well, I'll see what I can do."

He wrote several lines on a slip of paper, placed the paper in an envelope, and handed the envelope to Sergei, telling him to give the envelope to the Director of the Institute. "You will receive your stipend for the period which you missed. Return to school. Keep your eyes open. You will be contacted by someone who will tell you to whom to report. Now you will need this pass to get out of the building. Good day." He held out a signed slip.

Sergei was received back into the Institute immediately, and within a week was informed that his readmission into the Komsomol was under consideration. At the next meeting his case came up for discussion. The Secretary, Kolya, made an eloquent speech, organized around the theme that the Soviet state encouraged the rehabilitation of its citizens, and that they were pleased to have back in the Komsomol Comrade Kazetsky who had placed himself on record as being firmly opposed to his father's counter-revolutionary activities. This left Sergei nothing to do but stand up and denounce his father and disassociate himself from his family.

The next day he was contacted officially by the NKVD and given an address at which to report weekly with any information he might pick up which might be useful to the NKVD. The following week he made his first report. He carefully avoided telling anything incriminating, repeating only a few of the mildest of political anecdotes such as could be told almost openly. The resident agent to whom he reported said that he was sure that Sergei could discover more than this, and warned him that they would expect better results in the future. Sergei promised to do better.

Thus, suddenly, almost without knowing how, he had denounced his family and become one of the NKVD network of informers. What sort of a change had taken place in him? Really none, he told himself. He was only doing what was necessary and inevitable. He still believed his father to be the innocent victim of someone's mistake. "But what can a young boy do?" he would repeat in self-defense. "How else can I have a career? It is a necessary compromise. I will get out of this situation as soon as I can."

But there was no escaping.

Slowly at first, and then more rapidly, he found his relations with his fellow students changing.

Does he like me? Does he suspect me? . . . Such questions became a symphonic theme playing in the background of all his relations to people. And his own replies. . . . Shura dislikes me because I denounced my father, but he doesn't dare say so. Kolya treats me so respectfully because he thinks I am working for the NKVD. He really hates me. But why should he hate me? I am a decent fellow!

His doubts grew. He could no longer look inward upon himself for fear of what he would find there. He turned outward on the world, trying to find in the approval of others the respect he could not give himself. He became too eager to please, to be agreeable. He smiled habitually, almost in a simper, as if to say to the world: "I like you, I mean no harm, won't you accept me for the decent fellow I am, and like me too?"

But in reaching too hard toward other people he succeeded in pushing them away. The lack of genuineness intruded through the smile. Forced, almost frantic, speeches on "decency" and "honor" and "comradely relations" were greeted with bewilderment and bored silence by his comrades. Their coolness only spurred him to greater and more frantic efforts.

Suddenly he found in himself a violence that was difficult to control, and a bitterness that stemmed from loss of self-respect. His weekly reports became constantly more damaging. Kolya, the Secretary of the Komsomol, had been making derogatory remarks about "Party democracy"; a certain teacher had said that the great dams at Dnepropetrovsk could not have been built except with the help of American engineers; etc. He tried, he told himself, to be decent as long as he could, but if they rejected you, it was their own doing. He'd show 'em.

Kolya disappeared. One day he was there, making his eloquent, militant speeches, and the next day he was gone! It was rumored that he was arrested—that he had been part of a Trotzkyist group in the Komsomol. Turning in information is one thing, but having people arrested is another, Sergei realized. Surely it couldn't have been on the basis of my information that he was arrested. They must have had additional basis for suspecting him. After all, I only turn in facts. The responsibility for his arrest isn't mine. . . . It isn't! It isn't!

Sergei got drunk that night. He got drunk, and he got into a fight with a fellow student over some trivial issue. The issue didn't matter; it was as though he had to discharge his violence somewhere.

He began getting special assignments. He was told to become friendly with a new student, Nikolai Andreevitch Fedorov. Nikolai had a brother in the NKVD, and it had been said that he was talking too freely. Nikolai, being new, was glad to have a friend among the older students, and Sergei began dropping around to his house. One evening when he arrived, the older brother was there, in the uniform of an NKVD lieutenant—a stocky blond young man of about thirty, introduced as Yegor.

Yegor handed Sergei a bottle of vodka with a shaking hand. "Have a drink, have a drink!"

They drank steadily for about two hours. Yegor began getting more and more talkative, boasting at first of places he had been and girls he had had, and then of his influence, his drag with various people. As his speech began to thicken he bragged about the power of his uniform, how people quaked when they saw him coming. Nikolai seemed to be embarrassed at this turn of events, and tried to lead his brother back to more politically neutral topics: "Tell him about that blonde singer in Odessa, Yegor," he said. But nothing could stop Yegor. He went on, and started to curse some of the swine they had to deal with, remnants of the exploiting classes, obstinate pigs, who wouldn't own up to their crimes.

Suddenly he became silent, and seemingly morose. He poured himself several quick drinks in succession. Then they heard him muttering to himself: "That damned blood, take 'em away, take them all away. . . . I can't stand it. . . . Take 'em away!"

Nikolai and Sergei looked at each other in embarrassment. He must be joking, they thought, but this is nothing to joke about!

Yegor was fumbling with one hand beneath the table. "Where's the buzzer? Where's the buzzer?" He was looking for a buzzer button to summon an attendant. He looked around frantically, not seeing them, screaming, "Take him away, take him away!" He dove under the table, and began scratching feverishly at the underside in his search for the button. They stood off from the table, horror struck, unable to look away from him. Gradually he stopped screaming and thrashing, overcome with fatigue and the effects of the last several drinks.

They picked him up and put him on the bed.

Nikolai walked to the door with Sergei: "Seryosha, you won't tell anybody about this, will you?"

"Don't be stupid. What do you think I am, a goddam informer?"

"Of course not, but one must be careful. Good night."

Sergei walked back to his room slowly, greatly shaken. He said to himself: "It's all necessary work. I only turn in objective information. We must be on guard against enemies of the state and the program of the Party. . . ." He could see Kolya being interrogated, defending himself, protesting his innocence. To have to face a person in such a situation—to pass judgment—to squeeze from him an admission of what he denied—perhaps to exercise ruthlessness in extracting a confession! God, I couldn't ever do that! That horrible wreck of a Yegor—would I become like him? Sergei, Sergei, you have to get yourself out of this. . . . What is happening to you? Suppose they commandeered you to be a regular operator?

Should he report what happened? He was strongly tempted to do so, chiefly to observe the reaction of the agent who received his reports. What would he do, how would he look when Sergei told him of Yegor crawling and clawing and screaming? What repressed nightmares would it recall to the agent?

But when the time came to give his weekly report, he found himself completely unable to tell of what happened. It was as if hearing the description of it in his own voice would make the horror unbearably real. He merely said that he had met Yegor, that they had had a few drinks, and Yegor had talked about his girl friends.

"Good, keep at him. Try asking him next time a little about his work. Encourage him to talk."

It was the beginning of Sergei's last year in the Institute, and his studies were beginning to slip. He no longer found it possible to work effectively. When he was alone, he drank increasingly. But he tried to avoid being by himself, and became more and more occupied with political and social work. He tried to forget his feelings and fears by becoming immersed in day-to-day activity. But he had compromised too well. As a reward for his political activities, he was offered the opportunity of joining the Party. The "offer" he understood well as a directive. He made perfunctory noises about "not being sufficiently politically mature for so great an honor," but the Party secretary made it quite clear that candidacy was expected. So he became a Candidate for Party membership.

Then one morning he was notified that he had been selected for the NKVD training school in Kharkov. He inquired as discreetly as he could about the nature of such a notice, but only received confirmation of what he already knew. In view of the extensive purges which had been going on, the necessity for reliable persons in security agencies had increased, and the Party had decided to draft persons from its own ranks and the ranks of the Komsomol for training. There was no convenient escape. If you made excuses, they would counter them at every turn. "You have no choice, Sergei," he told himself again.

The following week he reported at NKVD headquarters to a Lieutenant Togorov. This was the first time since his initial contact with the NKVD that he had entered the headquarters building. As he walked up the long grey stairs he had the same queasy feeling in his stomach he had had the first time. The same routine with the papers and the guard, and finally he was ushered into an office. There were two men in the uniform of lieutenants sitting and talking. They stopped their conversation while the guard explained his business.

"Oh, yes," said one of the men, extending his hand and smiling distantly, "Comrade Kazetsky, we have been expecting you. I am Lieutenant Togorov, and this is Lieutenant Badinin. The guard will take you down the hall to a room where you will fill out certain forms. When you have done this, return here to us."

He was led immediately out to the office where he was given a long form that covered his life history in great detail, including his class origin, military experience, Party activity, education, occupation. When he had finished the form he returned to Lieutenant Togorov's office.

He sat uneasily while the two men looked over the completed form. His words might as well have been engraved in copper for all he could do to change them. His grandfather's saying kept running through his mind: "That which the pen has written, even the ax cannot chop out."

"Now, Comrade Kazetsky, we should like to ask you a few questions about your past. We must warn you that you are to answer these questions without reflection. We will consider hesitation as a false answer. Now, are you ready?"

"Yes, Comrade Lieutenant." But he knew he was not ready, and never would be. His stomach drew tight. He tried to relax and smile, but it felt as though his lips were twitching. What was there to be afraid of? He didn't know. Did they know about Yegor? Had he himself said something, let something slip when he was drunk? What about his father? Probably somebody had been reporting on him. . . .

"Your name?"

"Sergei Mikhailovitch Kazetsky."

"Place and date of birth?"

"Kharkov, 1918."

"Your father was arrested for counter-revolutionary activities?"

"Yes, Comrade Lieutenant, that is a matter of record."

He noticed that Lieutenant Badinin was scanning a dossier. The questions came from both sides, rapidly, covering every topic, and returning from time to time to the matter of his father's arrest.

"You were aware of your father's counter-revolutionary activities, and did not report them. Correct?"

"No, Comrade Lieutenant. I knew nothing."

"You must have been very unobservant. Did you know an engineer named Shmulokov?"

"Yes, Comrade."

"Did he ever visit your father?"

"Yes."

"Did you ever hear them discussing the strength of certain bridges over the Moscow river?"

"No, Comrade Lieutenant."

Oh, God, but I did. I remember it now. Can't change now. Keep a consistent story. . . .

Then a sudden shift.

"Why didn't you tell everything you observed about Yegor Fedorov?"

Was it a shot in the dark? Did they know something? Maybe Yegor had only been acting? He felt his fist clenched with the nails biting into the palms. For Christ's sake, answer the question! You've been standing there an hour. . . .

"But I reported everything. I met him once at his brother's. We had a few drinks. He bragged about what a great one he is with the ladies. Then I saw him no more."

Neither man said anything. Neither expressed any emotion.

After another half-hour the examination was finished. He was instructed to report on Monday, when his course of instruction would formally begin.

Later Sergei lay on his bed, trying to recall what he had said during the two-hour interrogation. He knew that it was vital to remember each word and each inflection as closely as possible. There would be other forms to fill out, other questions to answer, and you had to give the same story. You had a part to learn, and you had to learn it letter perfect, so that it came out swiftly, automatically, with no betraying hesitation and no revealing slips of detail.

On Monday, with thirty-five other students, Sergei began his formal training. From ten in the morning to eleven at night of the first day they went through their initial indoctrination. First a series of talks with interminable praise of Stalin and Beria. Then a briefing on the course and on their status. The course would last two years. They would receive 425 rubles a month, free meals, rooms, and uniforms, one month's vacation a year in October, and a week-end off every two weeks—an exceedingly good financial and material situation by standards of the thirties. They were again reminded that the government and their glorious Stalin were financing their training, and that their allegiance now lay only with their country and their leader. Family and friends were something of the past.

The dining hall at which they ate lunch was like nothing Sergei or most of the others had ever seen: freshly starched tablecloths, bright flowers on each table, waitresses bringing little baskets of white bread, borsch, large servings of meat with rice, jellies, coffee, and ice cream—all in any quantities one wanted. Cigarettes cost just about half of what they did in regular stores.

The students had their own recreation room with soft leather chairs, the latest magazines, books, and billiard tables.

Sergei shared a small but neat room with four others. The beds were all supplied with clean linen and plenty of blankets. It was a fairyland to Sergei. And from the otherwise bare walls there always looked down at him the pictures of Stalin and Beria.

The students were supplied with uniforms, had their heads shaved for lice. They were given more lectures, told again of their responsibilities, and reminded that henceforth they were to be ready for duty twenty-four hours a day.

At eleven o'clock they finally were dismissed, and Sergei slid between the freshly starched sheets, only to be awakened almost immediately by a strident bell and frightful commotion.

"It's a test drill! Hurry! Hurry!" he heard one of the other students explaining. Fumbling desperately he got into his clothes and ran out into the hall, buttoning his uniform with one hand and dragging his newly issued rifle and gas mask behind him with the other. Okay, okay, he thought, so I belong to the state, but do I have to be reminded of it in the middle of the night?

In addition to the incessant political indoctrination, all students were required to join various cultural circles for which trained instructors were provided. Sergei even learned to dance with a skilled teacher. He belonged to a choral group and was a member of a literary circle. Movies were shown in the auditorium several times a week, and from time to time groups were taken into town to see plays and attend concerts.

As the course proceeded through its first few months Sergei lost many of his old fears, doubts, and feelings of guilt. Not only was the life more pleasing and comfortable than anything he had dreamed of, but he was developing some feeling of oneness with his fellow students and with the instructors. Somehow he felt more secure now that he was clearly within the group that he had feared so much.

However, he was not entirely at ease. As the training proceeded he was called in from time to time for further oral questionings. There were always the same two smiling faces behind the desk, the freshly opened pack of expensive cigarettes, and the disarming questions. But in the midst of these disarming questions, he noticed that they returned time after time to many of the more sensitive topics about which they had queried him on the other occasions. Self-rehearsals stood him in good stead.

His first practical experience as an NKVD agent came after six months of schooling. One night, as so often, they were wakened about one o'clock. As they fell into line there was the same paunchy officer standing, watch in hand, timing them. "Good," he said. "Only six minutes." After pausing a moment, he continued: "Tonight, Comrades, you are not going back to sleep. You go on your first assignment. We have a list of counter-revolutionaries who must be arrested, and their apartments searched. You will go with experienced agents as observers."

The other students seemed excited. But Sergei had a sinking feeling. If they only knew. They must be really innocent. This is what I have been dreading and refusing to think about these months. . . .

The students were marched out into the yard, where about a dozen trucks were parked. Sergei was assigned to go with Lieutenants Gratinov and Pagrov, both of whom he knew slightly. Gratinov yelled out an address to the driver, and they were off careening through the almost empty streets.

Sergei sat silently next to Lieutenant Gratinov, trying his best to hide all emotion.

Gratinov broke the silence first: "Cigarette? Our first job is to take care of a capitalist pig that's been growing fat on the money he gets from foreign agents. He pretends to be only a carpenter, but he's built himself a big house."

Sergei nodded his head in assent, and gripped the sides of the truck as it screeched to a stop. As he climbed out, he saw the "big house," a shack made of old boxes and scrap wood, put together by hand.

The three men went around to the back. Gratinov banged at the door. At first there was no answer. Then they heard a woman's voice drowsily saying, "Just a minute." The door opened a trifle and a woman's sleepy face protruded.

"NKVD, we have papers to search your apartment," Gratinov shouted, and pushed the door open, stamping past the woman before she could say anything. Behind the wife Sergei saw the middle-aged husband and a son of about fifteen years old. The husband was barely awake, but he was repeating over and over: "We are simple people. We have done nothing." Gratinov and Pagrov began pulling out drawers, emptying shelves, searching for anything that might be politically incriminating. In their impatience they stepped on fragile articles, broke dishes, and tore clothes. The woman, more awake now, began to protest, while the man continued repeating his few phrases.

Sergei became panic-stricken. What are we doing? What have these people done? He looked at the boy, who was standing against the wall whimpering. Only half-consciously did he remind himself that this was virtually the same scene that had taken place in his own home. Finally he could stand it no more. The woman's voice tore at his guts. He spun around to her, and caught her across the mouth with his hand. "Shut up, you capitalist whore," he shouted. Pagrov looked up, slightly surprised, but seemed to approve. The woman stood silent, holding her hand over her mouth.

After half an hour of searching failed to produce anything, Gratinov shoved his rifle into the ribs of the trembling carpenter and said: "All right, get dressed and come along with us." They shoved and kicked him, still protesting, through the door and into the truck.

They completed three such assignments that night and returned to the NKVD compound about four o'clock in the morning. Other trucks were unloading prisoners and lining them up when they entered the yard.

The students were assembled, commended for their work, and dismissed for the night. Sergei noticed that most of them were pale and silent.

The next morning the students were told that they would observe the questioning of the prisoners arrested last night. A Lieutenant Yalik led the group of eleven in which Sergei found himself, into a small room without windows. The only furniture was a row of chairs for the students and a small table in a far corner.

When they were all seated, Lieutenant Yalik turned to them and said: "Remember, when you question a prisoner, it is not to find out if he is guilty. He would not be here if he were not guilty. Your job is to make him confess. If he doesn't confess, then *you* are guilty—of not doing your job. You must adapt your method of interrogating to the person with whom you are dealing. Now, for such hardened counter-revolutionaries as this group only the most drastic methods will work." He shouted to the guard, "Bring him in."

The guard shoved a bewildered, middle-aged peasant through the door. He hesitated as he stepped into the room. The guard gave him an additional shove with such violence that he stumbled and fell.

"Get up, you kulak pig," Yalik screamed, kicking him in the stomach. "Get up and confess."

The man drew himself to his feet, trembling. "What am I to confess to?"

"You know, you pig, you know. Confess."

Yalik motioned to the guard, who pushed the prisoner face up against the door. On the door was a sheet of paper about a yard square with rows of black dots covering its surface.

"Now," screamed Yalik, his face livid, "count those dots, you bastard, count and don't make any mistakes."

The man started counting. Sergei could see him straining to follow the mass of swarming black dots. Every time he hesitated or made a mistake, Yalik would kick him or whip him with a black belt that he twisted without end in his sweaty dark hands. "Start over again, you pig," Yalik screamed, dancing about the prisoner like a maniac. The scar on his cheek grew red, and saliva dripped from his thick lips. As the prisoner started counting again a guard from the outside would open the door with terrific violence, hitting the peasant in the face. This was repeated over and over again until he lost consciousness. Finally, he was picked up and taken away by a couple of guards.

Yalik spat on the floor and turned to the students, still shouting in the deathly still room. "You see, you see, that's how you must learn to question these hardened swine! He will confess. When he comes to, he will look at me and confess."

Sergei did not dare look at the other students. He hated himself. He said to himself: "Don't let it get you. You're not the one getting hurt. Remember your father. Do what you're told. They must be guilty of something." Again he practiced the answers he should give to the questions of others, to the point where he almost believed them. He began teaching himself a formula which he tried desperately to believe. He must deny all internal existence, and live in expectation of what his superiors demanded. His existence was in their eyes, in their anticipations, in their approbation.

The other students were doing the same. When they were on leave together, he noticed they never talked about their work and training. When they talked about school, they talked about the cultural circles, the pretty eyes of some waitress. They gripped the arms of their chairs until their hands grew white, as they smoked endless cigarettes, chewing at them feverishly as their mouths quivered.

Along with these new rules of conduct, Sergei found himself more and more concerned with the respect and privileges his uniform brought him. Everywhere he found obsequiousness, and the same eagerness to please that he himself manifested towards his superiors. If he entered a factory to see a friend, the director would be paralyzed with fright until he found the harmless nature of Sergei's business. Tram conductors didn't look at his little black permit book, but waved him in without paying. Store managers insisted that he take things at cut prices. His first astonishment gradually changed to anticipation of these acts of deference. He loved the power and importance of the uniform. The sacrifice of any inner life was compensated for by the outward symbols of power and importance on which he came to rely.

But the internal erosion could not be halted completely.

His first post after graduation from the NKVD school was as Junior Operations Officer in charge of a network of informing agents. Directly beneath him was a system of resident agents to whom the informers reported directly. His task was to maintain contact with the resident agents, meeting them at prescribed intervals at various rendezvous spots, and collecting the information they had gathered. It was also his responsibility to recruit and interview all prospective secret informers. His job, he realized, was exactly like that of Lieutenant Petrov, who had recruited him.

He was indoctrinated into the work by his immediate supervisor, Operations Officer Karodka. "The constant recruiting of new secret informers from every level of Soviet life is perhaps the most important job you will have," explained Karodka. "We have to meet norms set by the Oblast. They are putting pressure on us to exceed these norms by far. This afternoon you will watch me recruit an assistant bookkeeper from the local textile plant. We need him to get information about the director."

Sergei nodded. The recruiting of the assistant bookkeeper was a revelation to Sergei. The bookkeeper had not been told why he was wanted. When he was brought in he was puzzled and frightened. Karodka showed his big white teeth in an attempt at a friendly smile. He told the bookkeeper to sit down, offered him some very expensive cigarettes, talked about Stalin and the enemies of the state, then about the Capitalist encirclement. He asked the bookkeeper about his job, family, friends. Once again he talked about the glory of Stalin and about the Capitalist menace, then about the necessity of all good patriots to help their government. With these words, he paused, lit a cigarette and fixed his eyes on the bookkeeper. "Now yourself, Comrade Bzhevin," he said. "You're a patriot, aren't you?"

The bookkeeper hastened to protest his loyalty.

Karodka explained to him that the NKVD had unearthed evidence of counter-revolutionary activities at the textile plant where Comrade Bzhevin worked. There was evidence that even the highest people were connected with these activities. It would be possible to expose this menace to the Soviet government only with the help of patriots like Comrade Bzhevin. Thus, for him was reserved the great honor of doing something directly for the benefit of his country and proving his loyalty. Karodka also hinted that it would be useless to report that everything was all right since the NKVD already knew the contrary to be true, and thus Bzhevin would be guilty of concealing enemies of the state.

By this time Comrade Bzhevin was trembling visibly and wiping his perspiring face with his sleeve. Major Karodka smiled and continued, "Of course, we know that even a patriot needs a little time to think it over. So, Comrade Bzhevin, report back tomorrow and pick up your instructions."

After Bzhevin left, Karodka explained that he would be assigned to a resident agent who would direct his activities in the plant. Bzhevin would know no other agent except his resident director. "And naturally," said Karodka, "Bzhevin will be watched by another informer."

So this, then, is the way I was recruited. And I was informed on, too! . . .

Sergei found that recruitment into the network of informers had virtually nothing to do with willingness, even though a few people volunteered to inform—and those were mainly unreliable persons. He selected people on the basis of his needs, and then used whatever means that were necessary to get them in. A person who had been arrested, or who had had some relative arrested, was most susceptible to pressure. Such a person was told that becoming an informer was the only way he could prove his loyalty to the government. But if a man had a perfectly clean record, it was always possible to invent some blot with which to blackmail him. Sergei knew how. You could show him selected signed statements that he had committed some questionable act in the past. If you needed to search a man's apartment you engaged a hoodlum to accost him on the street and start a fight. Then they would both be arrested and kept in jail. During this time you could search his lodgings. If you didn't find anything compromising, you planted it and discovered it later as evidence to be used against him.

There were, however, differences in the extent to which people were compliant. In general it was foolhardy to resist, but it was amazingly difficult to get some people to agree. They never resisted openly, but they could be remarkably ingenious in thinking up excuses. And many who agreed on the surface actually did not cooperate. This could be told easily by the content of their reports, or from the reports of other informers. If the issue were important enough it was possible to bring almost anyone into line. In a few cases it was necessary to carry through on threats. In still fewer cases, when the situation did not warrant such drastic tactics, a particularly resistant person was let go after signing a statement that he would not reveal the contents of his interviews with NKVD personnel.

Sergei's day was flexible but full. He came to the office between ten and eleven and worked until one. From then until five-thirty he lunched, rested, and met with his resident agents. After that, until one in the morning, he worked, rested, ate, as circumstances demanded. When there were investigations and arrests to make he worked even longer hours. Sometimes he did not get to bed until morning.

Despite his unorthodox hours, he attended concerts, gave parties, and enjoyed a standard of living beyond anything he had ever dreamed of in his school days. He met an attractive dancer in a night club, and spent most of his free time with her. With his access to closed stores he was able to give her presents of clothing; and, by exerting influence in the right place, he arranged to get her a small apartment in a new building.

He took only a single room for himself, as he did not do any cooking, but he furnished it well and had a good short-wave radio and phonograph—and an excellent supply of liquor. It seemed possible at times almost to convince himself that he had a good life . . .

But the pressure of work, the ever increasing emphasis on filling norms for recruiting and for arrests, the fear that he was not doing a sufficiently good job, that he might be judged too lenient in the pressure he brought on agents, that he was not sufficiently ruthless in extracting confessions, the internal feelings of guilt and violence—all these began to gnaw away at the façade of confidence and self-control that he had derived from the power of his uniform.

Sergei found it difficult to remain still for even short periods of time. He paced about constantly and waved his arms. It was particularly disturbing when he tried to control this behavior and appear calm before prospective agents. He realized that sometimes he cut a queer figure—smiling too broadly, fumbling when opening a pack of cigarettes, walking excitedly about the room, raising his voice. Off duty he drank more and more, gulping down half tumblerfuls of vodka at a time.

He had been on the job for eighteen months. He needed a rest. All NKVD's did from time to time. He had been warned of this by observing his seniors. He applied for leave at an NKVD mountain sanatorium.

The month in which he was supposed to be recuperating did him no good. If anything, it made him worse. He had no patience with card playing, chess, walking in the mountains, any of the so-called "calming" activities in which he was encouraged to indulge. And the presence of old NKVD workers whose nervous condition had reached pathological proportions disturbed him all the more. Why did they keep these old wrecks around? This was supposed to be a place to rest!

Sergei became friendly with a Major who seemed more congenial and less disturbed than most of the senior officers. He and the Major went for walks together several times, had dinner in a local inn on two occasions, and spent a good portion of their evenings drinking together. They discussed literary problems, world politics, the local scenery, women—anything but work. The night before Sergei's leave ended the Major proposed that they have a celebration. They ordered a very elaborate dinner at the local inn, and each arrived with a bottle of vodka to top the event. They supplemented this with three bottles of wine. For hours they ate and drank. They went through a whole series of courses:

zakuski, pirogi, shchi, shashlik and rice, sweets and fruit for dessert, and between courses they toasted each other with vodka.

By the time the waitress had cleared away the last of the warm food and left them to munch on the fruit they were both maudlin drunk.

"Hate to see you go," said the Major.

"Hate to go, hate to leave you . . . hate to think of leaving you with nobody but all these old wrecks. They give me the creeps. When do you go back?"

The Major's face tightened. "Ten days, dammit. I have an interrogation to work on that's been going on for five months."

"Hm, you must be dealing with some important enemy of the state. He must be a tough cookie to deny his guilt so long."

The Major looked at Sergei with disgust. "Are you joking? What do you mean—deny his guilt? You know just as well as I do that half of these cases are frame-ups. The trouble is they want this guy for confession at a public trial. I know the kind of cases you've been working on—an obstinate kulak, some worker who couldn't keep his mouth shut, a young student who told too many political anecdotes—and you figure he has to be made an example of. Oh, I know your kind of interrogation. If they don't confess, beat 'em up. But that won't work with the cases I get. You have to sit down with these guys night after night until you go out of your mind. You have to persuade them by the most patient methods that they actually did what you know damned well they never did, or at most only thought of doing. Then the first thing you know, you *have* to get a confession out of 'em. Not because the head of your unit wants it, but because you need it to convince yourself. You know goddamned well that when you start to work on a guy you don't know whether he is guilty of anything or not, but you end up practically pleading with 'em to confess. Why do you think you hit those poor bastards you work over so hard? To stop your own doubts—that's why. . . . You're just like all of us. We're doing a stinking job we don't like, and we can't get out of it. Why do you think these old-timers are so goofy? Did you ever see one in really bad shape? Saw one go off his rocker in the middle of the office once, started shooting at a ghost in the corner.

Scared the crap out of all of us. . . . Wait till you been around awhile. . . ."

He lapsed into a moody silence.

This type of talk frightened Sergei. Was it a provocation? No, it didn't look like it. The Major was awfully drunk. God, what was this guy like? What were the rest of 'em like? Was everybody just caught up in some huge impersonal stream of circumstances that was carrying them on to some terrible fate? Does this guy understand any better than I do?

"There's something I don't understand," Sergei ventured. The Major continued to look morosely into his glass. Sergei thought: if it were a provocation he would encourage me. He said: "I recruit maybe a dozen persons a week. They don't want to come in. I didn't want to come in. I'll bet that nobody in my class wanted to come. Maybe one or two. Take you. We're all caught in the same way. How does it happen? I was completely loyal to the system even when I was an informer. It was just that I didn't like the work. Now it's worse. Is such work necessary? How many of these people are enemies of the system? How many of us feel the way I do? Doesn't anybody believe in what he's doing? Everybody I ever knew was blackmailed or conscripted."

The Major continued to gaze into the glass of vodka.

Sergei feared he had gone too far—that the Major was rebuking him by ignoring the question . . .

The Major glanced over at the remainder of the second bottle, picked it up, looked queryingly at Sergei to see if he wanted any. Sergei was too torn between fright and curiosity to respond. The Major evidently interpreted this as meaning that Sergei didn't want any. He put the bottle to his mouth, tipped it up, and drank all the vodka it contained.

"That's hard to say," the Major said, suddenly addressing himself directly to the question. "I got in during the early thirties because I was a homeless kid, and they raised me in one of the homes and made a good Party member out of me. Maybe you could say I 'believed' in what I was doing. I don't know. I think it was more that I just did what I was told. There were guys at that time, I suppose you might call them idealists after a fashion, who thought that the OGPU was really the guts of the Soviet system. They thought they were doing a dirty job that had to be done, a very important one, and I think they were really proud of it. These guys were really tough characters. They weren't like you and me. We have to be tough to keep ourselves from cracking up. But they were just plain tough. Those guys went out pretty early in the Yezhov purges. Now things are different. They're run on 'a business basis.' I suppose our capitalist friends would say: 'The NKVD doesn't want fanatics. They want guys who will do a job, and they'll do anything to get 'em to do it.'

"I know you're going to ask, 'Who's the NKVD if it isn't guys like you and me?' Well, I don't know. I imagine some place up the line you find people who believe in what they're doing. You even find a few on my level, I think, but it's awfully hard to tell. . . . Aw, Christ, what did we get into this crap for? Can't you find anything better to talk about? Come on, I know a waitress from the sanatorium who has her own room in town. Let's hunt her up. Maybe she can find somebody for you. Come, Seryozha, you're a good guy, I like you."

Sergei and the Major staggered out of the inn, arms about each other's waist. They found the waitress, who did indeed have a friend. Sergei was introduced to the girls. They sat about and talked for a few minutes until the Major strode over to the light cord and unceremoniously put out the light. In the gloom Sergei saw the Major put his arm about the waitress and pull her on to the bed. Her friend giggled; and Sergei kicked off his shoes. In the morning the Major was red-eyed and grouchy. He and Sergei kept the conversation on neutral, innocuous topics and parted very formally at the sanatorium. Sergei went to collect his things before leaving on the late morning train.

Sergei returned to work scarcely improved by his rest. The routine was pretty much the same—informers to recruit, midnight calls to round up counter-revolutionary elements, more questioning of prisoners. Sergei found himself shoving his rifle into the ribs of "capitalist pigs," bringing the butt of his gun down on their heads when they protested. In the interrogation rooms he yelled, "Confess, you swine," just as Yalik had done. At such moments he could not recognize himself as he danced about the prisoner screaming, kicking, striking, and wiping the saliva from his lips. Later, when he was alone, he would tell himself: "Yes, this is me. What it is necessary for me to be, I am!" Then he would grow angry with himself for even thinking about it. He would kick the prisoners all the harder, and would scream until he almost lost consciousness.

One morning his landlady said that a young man had been around to see him. She said she had told the young man that Lieutenant Kazetsky was in usually only in the early morning. He had said that he would return around ten o'clock. Sergei waited around impatiently. He had wanted to buy a pair of tickets for a concert that was being given that evening, and he had to be at the office by eleven. At last there was a knock. He walked to the door, and there was his old "friend" from the Institute, Nikolai, looking thin, shabby, and worried.

Nikolai smiled. "Hi, Seryozha."

"What do you want?" Sergei said suspiciously.

"I need some help. They arrested Yegor and now I can't get a job any place."

"Goddammit! What the hell are you coming around here for? I can't help you. That's your problem."

Nikolai's face hardened. "You have to help me. They are quizzing me about Yegor and they want to know about your relations with Yegor and me."

Fear ripped into Sergei. Christ, he thought, I knew I should have reported on Yegor.

"Well, don't hang around here, you jackass!" he exclaimed. "They may be shadowing you. . . ."

"They were," Nikolai cut in, "but I shook the bastard in the streetcar. That's why I was late."

"All right—now look, meet me at the Odessa Hotel at three o'clock this afternoon. And be sure nobody's following you there. Come up to Room 225, and do it without stopping at the desk or acting suspicious around the lobby." He watched Nikolai walking away and muttered: "You don't have to plant and cultivate fools; they grow themselves," not knowing whether he was referring to Nikolai or himself.

At three sharp Nikolai arrived and made his needs quickly clear.

He needed forged papers giving him a new identity, and he would leave town immediately.

"O.K.," said Sergei, "I'll prepare them myself. You meet me here at the same time, day after tomorrow."

But Nikolai did not appear on time.

When he had not arrived by three-thirty Sergei was certain something was wrong. Probably they had arrested him! Would he blab? Sergei took out the forged papers and carefully burned them piece by piece in an ashtray, placed the ashes in an envelope, and then flushed them down the toilet in the hall. Christ, now what can I do? he thought. . . .

He returned to the office. There was a message for him to report to a Colonel Medved at headquarters in the morning. He broke into a sweat as he read the message. He wanted to question the secretary about the note, but he stopped himself from doing so. It would be just another suspicious action to add to the chain of evidence. He must act as normally as he could. He must not look excited. He must . . .

He finished the day's work as best he could, went straight home, took two doses of a sedative, and proceeded to drink until the sedative took effect and he fell asleep. He awoke early, scared, unable to continue sleeping. He tried to eat breakfast at the canteen, but succeeded only in getting a cup of coffee down. He arrived at the Colonel's office fifteen minutes early.

The Colonel received him cordially, in fact unctuously. He smiled with a mouth full of tobacco-stained teeth, in the center of which was a single stainless steel one. The morning sun slanting in through the window glanced off the tooth, giving it a dazzling appearance that almost obscured the sight of the Colonel's face behind it.

"Well, Lieutenant Kazetsky, I presume that you would like to tell us the full story of your conspiratorial relationship with the brothers Fedorov?"

"Why, Comrade Colonel, there is nothing to tell. I don't understand."

"Well, Comrade Kazetsky," the Colonel smiled, "I'm sure you will remember what you are supposed to confess. You have been one of us too long not to understand. Go home, stand by your telephone until we contact you.   You are relieved of your duties."

Sergei went home with lead in his stomach.   He couldn't eat. He drank more than he ever had in his life, tumblerful after tumblerful, until he became violently ill.   After being sick he fell down on the bed and dozed off for a couple of hours.   About ten o'clock he woke up, half sobered but with a fierce headache.   He took a handful of aspirin and began drinking again. . . .

He poured the last of the vodka into the tumbler, and tried to shove the bottle into the waste basket.   It was too full, the bottle wouldn't go down.   It sat there on top with the light from the lamp reflecting off it, like the sunlight bouncing off the steel tooth of that blasted colonel.   The Colonel's mouth came swimming before Sergei.   It was smiling with the insinuating smirk that marked the professional inquisitor, and the words came out in a matching tone, flat and insinuating. . . .   "Well, Comrade Kazetsky, I'm sure you will remember what you are supposed to confess.   You have been one of us too long not to understand.   Go home, stand by your telephone until we contact you."

The bastard. . . .   Confess!   Confess!   What the hell can I confess?   I'll knock that goddam tooth down your throat—that's what I'll do.

He looked again at the light reflecting off the bottle.   He lunged over to the table, grabbed his service revolver, and brought the butt down on the bottle.   It burst into a myriad pieces.   He settled back in the chair, panting as though he had just escaped from the clutches of some evil being.

His thoughts raced on. . . .   But I can't get rid of the Colonel that easily.   How could I ever get in such a stinking mess?   Christ, what a mess!   I never did anything out of line.   I was always completely loyal.   All I ever wanted was to live decently, get along, stay out of trouble.   I did everything that was asked of me . . . I never tried to hurt anybody.   I'm a decent fellow. . . .   It was my old man, the bastard.   If he hadn't been stupid enough to get arrested, I would never have gotten into this position.   Everything dates to that night.   No warning, just that sudden loud knock, and the old lady stumbling in her sleep to open the door.   The old man bleating, "But I have done nothing, nothing I tell you, I am innocent.   I am completely loyal."

And the old lady protesting because they were tearing things apart, and the NKVD guy poking her in the mouth, to shut her up. . . . Then the silence after they dragged him out, and the beginning of the long road that got me here. . . .

So this is the progress you've made on the road that started with your father's arrest. . . . What a hell of a mess, Seryozha old boy. Sure, you always did what they asked you to—that is, almost. Why didn't you report on Yegor? Maybe you should have had more guts, told them to shove it when the old man got picked up, run off some place and changed your identify. . . . If it only weren't for that stupid old man, you wouldn't have had to compromise in the first place. . . . Well, you'll have to confess something. But they'll never be satisfied. They'll think you know more. . . . When the hell will they call? He looked at his watch. It seemed miles away, hazy. The edges wavered, melted, and then came back. He held it closer to his face—two-thirty—it's about time. . . . He hunted around for another bottle. Dammit, that must have been the last one. The phone rang. He started for it, fell against the lamp, putting out the light in the room. The phone rang again. The only light came in through the window from the street. Sergei staggered over to the table and slid his hand along the surface toward the phone. His hand hit something cold and hard. His revolver! He picked it up. The phone again! To hell with you, Comrade Colonel. . . . Sergei pressed the revolver against his head. . . .

Appendix

These portraits are attempts to present "typical" Soviet citizens in a variety of social roles. Although they are fictional in form, every effort has been made to insure the accuracy of their content. They are essentially an effort to present certain socio-psychological statements about the Soviet system in a concretized form. In a word, they attempt to show the pressures and rewards —the negative and positive sanctions the regime invokes—and the reaction of the Soviet citizen as he attempts to pursue his own goals within the framework that the regime has created.

The aim of these prototypes is to outline the "pattern of incentives and restraints" that characterizes the several roles depicted here and to indicate how a "typical" Soviet citizen responds to this pattern. To a great extent we find common underlying themes running through the various walks of Soviet life: the regime of terror effected by the secret police; the extreme pressure to work to the limit of one's powers; chronic material shortages for both producers and consumers; the all-pervasive politicization of life; the eternal trinity of Party, police, and administrative organs; reliance on extra-legal devices as ways around impasses posed by the over-rigid formal structure; the struggle of the individual to increase his sphere of free movement and his share of the limited material goods, and the regime's attempts to block him in this struggle.* Nevertheless, these themes tend to

* Despite the enormous expansion of Soviet industry, the citizens' share in

converge in different patterns for various roles, and each role has one or more characteristic features which it does not share with other roles. Thus the main task in describing these roles does not end with an enumeration of the factors involved; it is essential that the relative impact of the various factors be made explicit, and that the distinctive manner in which they are manifested be made clear.

Furthermore, because of the different demands that various roles place on people and the variety of life experiences, rewards, and negative sanctions that are associated with them, each role tends to attract—and retain—persons who possess certain traits of personality values, the ability to operate under circumstances of stress, the disposition to compromise one's principles vs. complete refusal to compromise, and so on.

The assumption behind the decision to present these prototypes in a fictionalized form, rather than as straight socio-psychological analysis, is that these patternings of personality and life situation can, for certain purposes, be communicated more effectively in the concrete form of the individual's behavior and subjective reaction in specific situations than in the more orthodox form of abstract analysis.

There are precedents for this method of communicating social psychological data. The most illustrious, probably, is Eileen Power's *Medieval People*. W. Lloyd Warner and Leo Srole included several such fictional portraits in their volume, *The Social Systems of American Ethnic Groups*. B. F. Skinner, in *Walden Two*, presents in fictional form the social implications of his system of psychology. No such attempts have, to my knowledge, been made in the Soviet field, except insofar as this is what every observant novelist does. For personality portrayals there are several such novels I would recommend. One is Igor Gouzenko's *The Fall of a Titan*. Another is *The Case of Comrade Tulaiev* by Victor Serge, which presents an excellent picture of the reactions and behavior of a group of highly placed people to the

the products of production has not risen nearly in proportion. Some writers have even argued that real wages actually decreased between 1928 and 1952. For a detailed assessment, see Janet Chapman, "Real Wages in the Soviet Union, 1928–1952," *Review of Economics and Statistics*, Vol. 36, No. 2, May 1954, pp. 134–156.

purges of the late thirties. In *The Time of the Assassins*, Godfrey Blunden does a similar study of behavior under German occupation in Kharkov. Blunden's *A Room on the Route* contains fictional portraits of a number of Soviet citizens in Moscow.

The main source of information on which these prototypes are based is the extended series of interviews with Soviet émigrés collected by the Harvard Refugee Interview Project, the data-gathering stage of the Harvard Project on the Soviet Social System, an Air Force sponsored research program.* In every instance there were in this series a minimum of a half-dozen interviews with persons who held one of the posts selected for analysis. Joseph Berliner, Mark G. Field, Sidney Harcave and Alexander Peskin deserve my gratitude for making available to me their interviews with former Soviet factory managers, doctors, and Party personnel.

The number of my colleagues to whom I am indebted is too long to be enumerated completely. Edward Wasiolek was, of course, a full-fledged collaborator. I must, however, mention Walt W. Rostow of M.I.T. for encouraging and supporting me in this project, the Center for International Studies at M.I.T. for generous financial assistance, and my friends and colleagues Clyde Kluckhohn and Alex Inkeles of Harvard, who were Director and Director of Research of the Project on the Soviet Social System. Richard Hatch was patient in tutoring me in some of the rudiments of writing fiction.

The material of the Harvard Project was supplemented by standard non-fictional sources, both Soviet and non-Soviet, by study of Soviet fiction, and by my own contact and interviews with Soviet émigrés while I was field director of this project in Europe during 1950–51. In virtually all cases (with the exception of the portrait of the NKVD agent) it was possible to verify by careful reading of Soviet sources the evidence gained from interviewing Soviet émigrés.

A cardinal principle of these prototypes is that the fictional vehicle must be subordinate to the sociological points to be made. In order to preserve the authenticity of these sketches, I have tried

* Done under Contract AF 33(038)—12909.

almost exclusively to borrow or adapt incidents from interviews, from Soviet fiction, from journalists' accounts, or from official Soviet sources. Changes were made only for the purpose of relating factual material more coherently to the over-all framework. In some cases, however, a considerable amount of inference had to be drawn. For example, the data on the subjective life of the secret police agent is very sparse. His feelings and emotions had to be inferred from accounts we have had of the behavior of such agents, and from what interviews with a few persons who admitted working with the secret police tell us of their personalities. Even here, however, the bulk of the material is based on direct evidence, and all of the main incidents come from reliable published and interview sources.

In certain instances the unity of the fictional vehicle demanded the invention of incidents which, though plausible, could not be directly verified. The instances are few. The limiting case is the sketch of the Soviet author, in which the success of his book depends on the misinterpretation by the critics of his essentially anti-Soviet symbolism. In this case I feel that the incident is poetically accurate, even though it would be difficult to prove that such an incident has actually ever occurred. Anyone who has followed the ins and outs of Soviet criticism and Soviet intellectual life over the years, with the intricacies of argument and reversals of line that go into defining what is officially approved at any one time, and has observed desperate attempts to stretch a mole hill of information into a mountain of conclusions, must have felt, as I have, that occasionally someone with his tongue in his cheek has deliberately slipped a bit of heresy past the bedeviled censor. In any event, the reader is properly warned of this instance of poetic license, and assured that all other incidents are closer to established fact.

How can a single person represent *the* Soviet factory manager, *the* Soviet tractor driver? Clearly the selection of one among various types of persons and behavior who may characterize a given role is, in itself, a crucial decision. In every instance there have been two or more modalities between which to select. I have tried to select the major mode and, when there was doubt, to give preference to the type which represented the newer trends in the system. In all instances I have tried to indicate variability by the introduction of alternate minor types, or by suggesting alternate forms of reaction which were possible for the person being portrayed. In the case of the students, a point in the system where heterogeneity is particularly marked, I have used not one, but three central characters.

The decision as to what general points should be made about each role involved complications. To some extent the task of these prototypes is to communicate points which are characteristic of the Soviet system as a whole; but to an equal degree they are intended to convey what is characteristic of specific roles as distinguished from others. I have *tried* not to weight the presentation in either direction, but in all probability there is actually something of a tendency in these prototypes to stress the differences rather than the uniformities.

A further complication lies in the relative emphasis that should be given to the distinctly Soviet aspects of the various roles. The reader will discover many familiar personalities and many familiar situations in these sketches—familiar on the basis of his own experience in American life. The reason is simple: the Soviet Union is a modern industrial society (or is at least in the last stages of becoming one), and all industrial societies have many features in common. Having these features in common, they also select out quite similar personalities to fill their various functions. There is much in the life and person of the Soviet factory manager that is like that of the American industrialist. There are considerable similarities between Soviet doctors, writers, students, and their American counterparts. Many of the rewards and problems which the Soviet citizen experiences are identical with those experienced by his "opposite number" in most western societies. These sketches emphasize the characteristically Soviet aspects of these roles, but it would be unfortunate if this led to an underestimation of the basic similarities which underlie all modern industrial societies.

Ideally one would describe a very large number of role-types from the Soviet system. But, granting limitations of time and information, some decision had to be made as to which half-dozen or so roles should be studied. The choice fell rather heavily on the middle ranks of the elite. For understanding problems of social control in the Soviet Union this is the crucial group. It takes little imagination to understand why the member of the Politburo or the Central Committee of the Party remains on the job. His degree of commitment to the system is so great that in most cases it must be assumed that he sees his interest as identical with that of the Soviet State. Similarly, on the other end of the continuum, the rank and file worker and peasant present relatively uncomplicated pictures. They have comparatively little freedom of movement or choice, and little need to take initiative. This is not to say that either extreme, the very highly placed or the very lowly placed, is not interesting and important to study, but merely that in a system of priorities they would come somewhat lower than the middle group. This latter group is characterized by the fact that it is not always highly politicized; the primary commitment of its members is not exclusively to the system *qua* system, but they respond rather to a pattern of more limited incentives, personal motives, stimuli, controls, and pressures. Furthermore, their contribution to the functioning of the system is so crucial, and the degree of skill and initiative required of them so considerable, that control and motivation of their role behavior is a matter of life or death to the system as a whole. Within this group the roles selected—the factory manager, the doctor, the secret police agent, the student, the tractor driver, the creative artist, the housewife, the woman collective farmer, and the Party secretary—were chosen so as to offer a maximum range of situations.

It seems to me that a question which will arise in the minds of many readers is that of whether the picture of Soviet life drawn here is dated by developments since Stalin's death. While there is by now fairly clear evidence that the new regime has adopted tactics somewhat different than those of Stalin, there is little indication of changes in the essential nature of Soviet life. This may come in time, but even if the promises of the new regime were to be taken on their face value, they could be fulfilled only over a period of years.

The Students

Whereas a process of selection has clearly been at work by the time a person takes any of the adult roles depicted in this series, the life of the student precedes somewhat the most crucial selection processes in the Soviet system. Hence the degree of heterogeneity in the student population is quite marked. I have focused on three (and a half) persons. The "hero," Stepan, is a studious scholar; the "New Soviet Man," Pavel, is an opportunist; Nina is the prototype of the "Komsomolka," the serious, politically active young woman student; Vera is the type of girl who may be found in school anywhere—primarily interested in men and social life.

Despite the fact that the type of school depicted here, a pedagogical institute, is less political than the average Soviet institution of higher education, the role of the Komsomol in student life is considerable, and the students are organized to do social and political work outside the school.

In the life of the student the warmth of interpersonal relationships and of comradeship is one of the sources of greatest immediate personal satisfaction. Notwithstanding the atomization of interpersonal relationships that tends to be produced by an atmosphere of constant suspicion in the Soviet system, student life is marked by strong warm friendships that seem to spring from the basic values of Russian culture.

Good descriptions of modern Soviet student life (with the expected Soviet slant) can be found in two untranslated Soviet novels: Iurii Valentinovich Trifonov, *Studenty* (The Students), Moscow, 1951; and V. Dobrovolski, *Troye v Serykh Shinyelyakh* (Three in Grey Capotes), Moscow, 1949.

The Woman Collective Farmer

Particularly since the war, women have comprised a majority of the ordinary field hands on the collective farms, and this group is the most poorly rewarded and most exploited of any except the residents of forced labor camps. The woman collective farmer has the least attractive life of any of the rank-and-file Soviet citizens. She is bothered by most of the problems that trouble everyone else—the police terror, the boredom of constant political indoctrination—but they fade into the background because of the extreme urgency of her central problem of making a living. A former Soviet tractor driver commented to us: "On the collective farm they go around in torn clothes. Oh, I wish I could lead you into a peasant's hut. You would say, 'There are pigs living here.' The first thing that would strike you was the smell. The women work all day. There is no time to make 'culture.' " The private plot of the peasant becomes the focus of his life. If he can get himself a large enough plot, and devote enough time to cultivating it, he can subsist reasonably well. The regime has waged a constant battle—not always entirely successfully—to restrict the size of the peasant's plot, and to get him to spend a maximum amount of time working for the collective farm.

Theft of collective farm property and irregular uses of property and produce is a regular event, and takes place among persons on all levels. Among the field hands, such thefts often spell the difference between subsistence and perishing. Even in the postwar period there has been at least one year in which there was actual starvation in the rural areas. Even in such periods, the government tries to exact a maximum amount of grain for distribution in the cities. The administration of the farm, while formally identified with the government, actually finds itself caught between two forces. The chairmen of collective farms are acutely aware of the need for maintaining a minimum of good morale among the workers on the farm, and very obviously frequently see themselves as being in conflict with "the Center." There is widespread evidence of evasions of grain delivery schedules by chairmen caught in these pincers. Because the problem of surveillance is more difficult in rural areas, such irregularities are even more pervasive than they are in the cities.

Peasant women have always been noted for their uninhibited speech. Since the war, with a shortage of men in the villages, this seems also to be accompanied by a similar progressive relaxation of sexual inhibitions. The speech and behavior of the women in this story are by no means overdrawn.

Vera Panova, who has succeeded in writing some surprisingly realistic novels about Soviet life, deals with postwar life on a collective farm in her *Yasni Bereg,* translated as *Bright Shores* in

Soviet Literature, 1950. Such stories, however, give no picture of the dreariness and drabness of peasant life, and of the extent of thieving on the collective farms.

The Woman Doctor

Whereas the factory manager is responsible for the output of material goods, the doctor is responsible for the soundness of the human material who operate the system. In comparing the attitude of the regime toward engineers and doctors, Soviet émigrés remark caustically, "You get paid according to the value of the material you work with." The doctor is next to the lowest paid of professionals; only school teachers are lower. The cream of Soviet manpower is encouraged to go into other work, and in recent years it has become something of a matter for apology for a male student to enter medical school, such an action being interpreted as an indication either that he had not the ability to become an engineer, or that he is politically unreliable. This is largely the explanation of the fact that since the Revolution the proportion of women doctors has risen from ten percent to over seventy-five percent. Medicine is also the least politicized of the professions. Perhaps fewer than twenty percent of doctors are members of the Party. These Party members are almost exclusively medical administrators. The administrators, in turn, are also predominantly male. The pattern which is evolving is that of a medical profession which is composed of non-Party, female, practicing physicians, and Party, male, medical administrators.

A further important aspect of the medical role is the extent to which the doctor becomes the focus of certain conflicts of interest of the state and the citizen. In addition to healing the sick, he is an agent of social control. It is, for example, his responsibility to decide when a person is or is not well enough to work. He is under pressure from workers to excuse them from work, and under pressure from the regime to reduce the number of absences from work. At times there have been quotas on the number of excuses a physician could issue, and occasionally excuses have been completely forbidden for brief periods in production and harvest crises. Here, and in other areas of medicine, it is clear that

Soviet medicine is oriented primarily toward the interest of the system, and secondarily toward the interest of the citizen.

Despite political interference in medicine and chronic shortages of material and equipment, the traditional values of the physician assert themselves. The Soviet doctor clearly sees his own responsibility as primarily to the patient, and continues to act in this way.

One point should be made very strongly: both doctors and patients, judging by attitudes expressed in interviews, seem to approve very strongly of the Soviet system of socialized medicine. It is only interference with this system, and failure of the regime properly to implement it, that they criticize. This situation combined with the obvious identification of the physician with the interests of his patient make him the professional most highly esteemed by the people, even though the regime does not grant him the same value. And, despite the conflict which certain of the regime's demands engender, he seems to derive as much personal satisfaction from his work as anyone in the system—and considerably more than most.

As indicated above, much of our knowledge of the situation of the Soviet doctor comes from a series of interviews with former Soviet doctors carried out by Mr. Mark G. Field, of Harvard University, and his subsequent analyses of these interviews, combined with a close reading of official Soviet journals dealing with medical problems, and medical administration. His published work on this subject includes: "Workday of the Soviet Physician," *New England Journal of Medicine,* February 4, 1954; "Some Problems of Soviet Medical Practice: A Sociological Approach," *New England Journal of Medicine,* May 28, 1953; "Structured Strain in the Role of the Soviet Physician," *American Journal of Sociology,* Vol. LVIII, No. 5, March 1953.

The Party Secretary

There is probably no figure in Soviet society about whom it is harder to write than a member of the Party "apparat." Virtually every Soviet novel contains a Party secretary. He seems to be a compulsory minor character without which a manuscript cannot pass the censor. Yet he is inevitably badly drawn, stiff, wooden, and flat. Perhaps there is a deliberate pact between Soviet writers and Soviet reviewers, whereby the reviewers always have something about which they may criticize the author, and thereby withhold their critical fire away from more essential aspects of the novel.

There are certain things about a Raion secretary about which we can be quite sure. His is actually much less of a political being than the Western notion of an "Official of the Communist Party" would suggest. He is a combination of administrator, technician, and trouble shooter. He is the Party's representative, who in the name of the Party must do everything in his power to keep *all* affairs in the Raion running according to the Party's designs. One of his main concerns is the industrial and/or agricultural production of his region.

The chances are strong that he will have had a technical education, have become a member of the Party apparatus while fairly young, and worked himself up in the ranks. Like the factory director, he is given to "localism." While he is supposed to represent the "Center," he also develops a good deal of identification with the region. He often fears that directives from the "Center" will destroy the delicate balance of forces that he is trying to keep under control. He is more responsive to the demands of people under him than the Center would like, and less responsive than they would like.

He seems to be a very much overworked and overextended man, with far more to do than should be expected of anyone. (But here I may be falling a victim of Soviet novels which stress this point *ad nauseam*.)

Politics are an appendage on his main job, which he sees as mainly one of bureaucratic administration. But politics are something he must pay attention to. He is responsible for the morale and political education of the Raion. He supervises the Raion newspaper, organizes propaganda and agitation campaigns, and is answerable for the political education of inductees into the Party and Komsomol. Party policies come down from above. He does little more than try to understand them and carry them out as best he can. Certainly he has no voice in shaping them, and it is doubtful that he bothers to question them.

He is also caught up in organizational politics, and this can occasionally be a matter of vital concern to him. "Proteksiia" (protection) is a *sine qua non* for advancement and safety in the Soviet bureaucracy. But, having a powerful protector inevitably means being involved in internal factional strife. When powerful figures in the Party jockey for position at the top of the hierarchy, the reverberations are felt down in the lower strata of the "apparat." In such instances, men in the lower echelons must indeed regard the impact of higher level power struggles as a *deus ex machina,* as a set of entirely external forces over which they have no control, the direction of which they cannot predict from moment to moment. These events must be regarded by them as unpleasant intrusions which are not a regular part of their job.

It is the more intimate and informal details of the life situation of the Party secretary on which we are ignorant. Soviet novels and Soviet official literature (with a few exceptions) present so stereotyped a view of the Party secretary that they contribute little to our understanding of these problems. Among our own interviews, we have only a half dozen or so with persons who were actually in the Party apparatus, and they are not particularly rich in this sort of information, since they were directed mainly at the more technical details of Party organization and function. I have had to guess at what a Party secretary would think and how he would act in the kind of political crisis portrayed in this story. His behavior toward other persons with whom he deals is quite well described by many of our respondents, but, again, we guess at what goes on in his mind when he behaves in this fashion. It is for these reasons that I feel that, more than in the case of the other stories, the Party Secretary has some of the wooden flatness of his counterpart in Soviet novels.

Good published sources giving a realistic picture of the Party Secretary are rare. The functioning of the local Party apparatus is discussed by Merle Fainsod in Chapter Eight of *How Russia Is Ruled,* Harvard University Press, 1954. Three documents prepared as part of the work on the Harvard Project on the Soviet Social System proved very helpful. They were: Sidney Harcave, "Structure and functioning of the lower Party organizations," mimeo., 148 pp., Cambridge, August 1953; Vera S. Dunham, "The local Party secretary in Soviet literary sources," 164 pp.; Vera S. Dunham, "The Party secretary in post-war Soviet literature," 83 pp., mimeo., Cambridge, August 1953.

The Housewife

The Soviet housewife is as often as not also a working woman. Since the early thirties real wages have gone down to the point where the family unit needs the earnings of every member who can work. "Grandma" therefore plays an important part in the family, since she can take care of the children, keep house, and stand in queues. Despite the well-publicized system of crèches for the care of children of working mothers, it appears that a large proportion of mothers do not use such facilities. In many instances (as testified to by complaints in the Soviet press) the proper authorities neglect to build crèches, and in other instances the family is reluctant to bear the cost of having the child taken care of there. Our own data indicate that only a minority of Soviet urban families actually have the benefits of grandma's presence. Yet, when she is available she is almost invariably welcomed as a contributing member of the family rather than as a charge on the family. The presence of some member of the older generation who is available to carry out the household responsibilities is an integral part of the ideal Soviet family.

The actual physical conditions of family life in a Soviet city are a little difficult for an American to comprehend. In the larger cities even the families of professional men are likely to regard themselves as fortunate to have one good room in an apartment, and share the kitchen and bathroom with other tenants of the same apartment. Buildings are not kept in repair. One or two disagreeable persons can make life difficult for everyone else. Electricity is (or has been) rationed. Cooking may be done over a small, portable stove in the corner of the living room. Heating is likely to be poor, or the heating plant may be broken. By and large, the living conditions of the family depicted in the story of the housewife are better than average for a person of this status in any large Soviet city.

The family circle is the place where the Soviet citizen probably finds his greatest happiness.   Family relations are generally quite warm.   The main complaints of the Soviet citizen about family life is the extent to which the drudgery of making a living interferes.   He is resentful of the time he has to spend away from the family, and the degree of fatigue with which he returns home. Despite—perhaps because of—the difficulties of making a living, Soviet mothers and fathers are anxious for their children to become educated and get a good job.   This is true regardless of how the parents feel about the regime itself.   They want a "career" for their children, and especially for their boys.

The Writer

The next sketch is of the creative artist—the novelist, poet, playwright.   The favored members of this group enjoy a higher standard of living than anyone else in the Soviet system, including possibly the very peak of the ruling elite.   For no group does the degree of compromise seem greater.   Not only must the artist create according to a prescribed pattern, but the limitations set on the Soviet artist are such that creativity, regardless of the content of the message, is stifled.   Even if he accepts this compromise he never feels entirely safe, since the definitions of what is politically desirable in the world of art are not only extremely ill-defined, but they change from time to time with dramatic suddenness.

Recognizing the nature of artistic work, and the temperament of the artist, the Soviet regime has stressed positive incentives more in this than in any other role.   Negative incentives, threat of police action, exile, deprivation of the opportunity to work within one's profession, are all present, but they are crucial in the lives of only the lower ranks of artists.   It is the promise of very high royalties, of a good apartment, of several motor cars, that motivates the top-flight artist to bend his talents to the state.

It must not be assumed that every top-flight Soviet artist has "sold out."   The evidence seems to indicate very strongly that many of the best writers, musicians, graphic artists, attempt simultaneously to satisfy their artistic principles and retain the favor of the regime.   This image I have tried to convey in this sketch.

As incredible as it may seem, the scene in which the venerable scholar is abused because his collection of folklore does not reflect enough credit on Stalin is adapted from an actual incident observed by Robert Magidoff, and reported in his *In Anger and Pity*, New York, 1949. Virtually every other point made in this story can be documented several times over from *Taming of the Arts*, by Juri Jelagin, New York, 1949.

The Factory Director

The Soviet factory manager is the one person on whom the regime relies most heavily for the production of goods. He is judged, rewarded, and punished primarily on his ability to meet and beat production quotas. His handicaps are: chronic shortages of materials, bureaucratic red-tape, constant surveillance by the secret police, and political interference by the Party. The contribution of the Ministry, the MGB, and the Party is not always negative, but they do present a constant source of inhibition on the initiative which he would like to take. He, himself, is usually a Party member, being one of those "responsible workers" that the Party recruits into its ranks in order to extend the area of its control over him.

The manager is repeatedly faced with "impossible" situations, but since virtually no excuse is acceptable from a responsible Soviet worker, he is compelled to find some way of accomplishing the impossible. To a great extent this is accomplished by informal and extra-legal maneuvers which operate outside of, and frequently contrary to, standard operating procedures. These unorthodox devices are obviously known by the authorities and, if kept within limits, seem to be tolerated as long as production is kept up. One of his gambits, to keep production quotas as low as possible so as to maximize the factory's (and his own) profits, is resisted, however, by the regime.

If he is successful he is well paid and receives production premiums. He has a great deal of prestige and power—virtually an empire of his own—and he enjoys a standard of living second only to a few extraordinarily privileged groups. If he fails he is demoted, and in extreme cases may face political charges. In general, both the sanctions invoked by the regime and the outlooks of the manager have become more economic and less political since the mid-thirties. The tendency of the manager to look at problems from the more narrow industrial frame of reference and give priority to the interests of "his" firm over the interests of the state has come in for repeated criticism.

Vera Panova, again, gives a many-sided picture of a factory director in her novel, *Kruzhilika,* published in Moscow in 1948, and translated into English as *The Factory,* London, 1949, Putnam. Joseph Berliner's doctoral dissertation, *The Soviet Industrial Enterprise,* Harvard, 1954, furnished the main basis for this sketch.

The Tractor Driver

The tractor driver is distinguished from the mass of the peasantry by his somewhat better income, his prestige as a man who works with machinery, his more than average initiative, and a level of education that by no means all of the younger peasantry have obtained. If his ability and initiative warrant it, and he stays out of trouble, he will become a brigadier on the Machine Tractor Station, or will move on to a factory job in the city.

The Secret Police Agent

The secret police agent is a marginal case in which many of the essential aspects of the regime manifest themselves in exaggerated form. Of crucial importance is the manner of recruitment. Particularly since the mid-thirties—the universal turning point in all the highly political areas of Soviet life—the emphasis has been on recruiting persons who could be depended on to "do a job" reliably out of self-interest, rather than convinced idealists. The type of person who volunteered to do secret police work out of conviction of its political necessity seems to have disappeared from the ranks of the MGB. Those who now enter into this work are largely those over whom the secret police or the Party have some lever of coercion. Sometimes they are Party or Komsomol members assigned this duty as a "Party responsibility." In other instances they are persons compromised either by their own activities or associations.

From interviews with a number of persons who admit having worked regularly for the secret police, and on the basis of more general knowledge, it is possible to infer with a fair degree of reliability the type of person toward which the members of the secret police are currently weighted. (This statement, it must be remembered, does not refer to the higher echelons.) Such persons tend to be compromisers, generally with little pronounced chance of succeeding in more technical work either on the basis of ability, or capacity to work effectively. Further, they have a very poorly defined self-conception, and little in the way of moral resources to fall back on. Their particular conflict lies in the fact that, lacking any standards of their own for judging their behavior, they find it particularly threatening to turn against their fellow-men and spy on them. They seek the approval of the very people they destroy.

The regime gives them very generous material rewards by Soviet standards. They derive satisfaction from their own sense of power. Nevertheless, they seem, as a rule, to disintegrate under the strain of their work. Drinking off duty is heavy. Psychiatric breakdowns seem to be very frequent. They do impulsive things under the pressure of their own internal distress, and these actions often get them in trouble with the regime. The specific incident which brings about "Sergei's" downfall is adapted with very little change from a story told by an ex-NKVD agent as happening to himself.

The sketch presented here is cast in the period of the great purges. This was done because of the difficulty of getting authentic data on post-war activities of the secret police. Enough is known, however, to assure me that the essentials of the picture painted here have not changed.

Reliable information on the operation of the secret police is hard to come by despite the plethora of descriptions of certain of their activities, such as techniques of interrogation. In addition to a number of interviews which we had with former members of the secret police, the following sources were relied on: "Shkola Oprichnikov" (The School of Inquisitors), A. Brazhnev, "Possev," Nos. 17–35 from April 29 to September 2, 1951; *Stalin's Secret Service,* W. G. Krivitski, New York, 1939; *I Spied for Stalin,* Nora Murray, New York, 1951; *NKVD,* B. B. Pozdynakov, Document, Harvard Russian Research Center; *Activities of Organs of*

State Security in the Soviet Union, V. P. Artemiev, Document, Harvard Russian Research Center.

Our description of the NKVD training school follows closely that of Brazhnev. Many of the incidents including the circumstances of Sergei's recruitment, the hallucinations of the drunken NKVD agent, and, as mentioned above, the conditions under which Sergei finally got in trouble were taken from the life stories of our respondents.

The actual methods which Mr. Wasiolek and I used were these: When a particular role type had been selected, we would hold a conference in which we would decide what broad points should be made (always being prepared for some alteration in these points as our work proceeded) and what sorts of materials could be used to provide the information we needed. He would then proceed to collect raw material for the portrait that was to follow. Invariably it would mean locating and assembling, from the many hundreds of interviews which we had, all those which had been done with anyone who had actually occupied such a position in Soviet society, or who had been closely enough associated with it to be a good observer of it. Then he would go through contemporary Soviet fiction looking both for information which would cause us to expand or revise our main themes, and for illustrative incidents which Soviet and other writers had used to convey such themes. After this, he would do the necessary reference work, running down those technical details of Soviet life about which he or I felt unsure. In fully half the cases, he also prepared a draft story which served as a vehicle for conveying a variety of illustrative incidents. My heavy work began at this point. I would spend a week or so reading interviews, going over the raw material he had collected from Soviet sources, and going back to standard works on the Soviet Union until I felt that I not only was clear on the technical details, but also that I had caught the "feel" of the particular role with which we were dealing. Then I would try to devise a story line which would permit me to make all of the essential points. As indicated above, I tried to stick as closely as possible to the use of incidents or stories which were derived from the real situations, modifying them sufficiently to fit into the general line of the narrative. In some instances I stuck fairly closely to the general framework of Mr. Wasiolek's draft, even though departing from it considerably in detail. While he deserves much credit for his contribution to these stories, he deserves little blame for their final form.

Glossary

batushka Affectionate diminutive for "dad" or "old man."

dacha Summer house.

diamat. A contraction for dialectical materialism, the Soviet official philosophy.

domuprav Building superintendent.

feldsher A medical assistant somewhat better trained than a nurse, who in some areas is still a main source of medical aid. He occasionally performs minor operations in the rural areas.

kasha Barley porridge.

kino The cinema.

kolkhoz Collective farm.

kolkhoznik Male collective farmer.

kolkhoznitsa Female collective farmer.

Komsomol Young Communist League.

kopek Coin of little value.

kulak A well-to-do peasant. The term literally means "fist."

MGB Ministry of State Security, the most recent of the names for the secret police.

MTS Machine tractor station.

muzhik A peasant.

NEP Period of the New Economic Policy, a period of partial reversion to capitalism in the twenties.

NKVD The people's Commissariat of Internal Affairs, the name which the secret police held up to the end of World War II.

Obkom   Oblast Party Committee.

oblast   A large administrative district but smaller than a republic.

OGPU   An early term for the secret police.

partorg   Party organizer.

pirogi (pirovka)   Heavy pastry stuffed with meat.

Raikom   Raion Party Committee.

raion   Minor administrative district immediately under the jurisdiction of the oblast.

RAPP   The Russian Association of Proletarian Writers, a group which militantly espoused the extension of political control over the arts.

shashlik   Skewered lamb.

shchi   Cabbage soup.

Spetsotdel   "Special Section," a division of the secret police.

tekhnikum   A technological institute.

Trotzkyist   A follower of Leon Trotsky.

Village Soviet   Local elective governing body, which carries out many bureaucratic functions, but is not the effective source of power in the area.   Political power resides in the local Power unit.

Yezhov   Head of the secret police in the mid-thirties, who was responsible for the most drastic of the purges.

zakuski   Hors d'oeuvres.

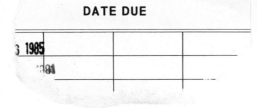